To: Kevin
From: Terry
with much love
12/93

warrior
wisdom

warrior wisdom

"Seek not to follow in the

footsteps of men of old;

seek what they

sought."

—Matsuo Basho
Seventeenth-century
Japanese poet

Compiled
by
Daniel Moore

RUNNING PRESS
PHILADEPHIA, PENNSYLVANIA

Canadian representatives: General Publishing Co., Ltd.,
30 Lesmill Road, Don Mills, Ontario M3B 2T6.

International representatives: Worldwide Media Services, Inc.,
Worldwide Media Service, 30 Montgomery Street, Jersey City, New Jersey 07302.

9 8 7 6 5 4 3 2 1
Digit on the right indicates the number of this printing.

Library of Congress Cataloging-in-Publication Number 93-83457
ISBN 1-56138-312-0

Cover design by Toby Schmidt
Interior design by Robert Perry
Cover photograph by Jeff Corwin
Edited by David Borgenicht
Typography: Garth Graphic, with Bodega Sans, by Richard Conklin

This book may be ordered by mail from the publisher. Please add $2.50 for postage and handling.
But try your bookstore first!
Running Press Book Publishers
125 South Twenty-second Street
Philadelphia, Pennsylvania 19103-4399

Dedicated to men of every stripe.

Let Us Be Men

For God's sake, let us be men
not monkeys minding machines
or sitting with our tails curled
while the machine amuses us, the radio or
      film or gramophone.

Monkeys with a bland grin on our faces.

—D. H. Lawrence

Acknowledgments

Thanks are due to my wife, Malika, and my two children, Farid and Saliha, for their patience while I wrestled this book to the ground. Thanks also to Sally Blaufuss, bookseller, for her boundless generosity, and to my editor, David Borgenicht, for his care and enthusiasm.

contents

Trying to define yourself is like trying to bite your own teeth."

The English Zen scholar Alan Watts once said, "Trying to define yourself is like trying to bite your own teeth."

In the very midst of being men, we are in an era of redefinition. As men we exist in a society that is not quite sure what to do with us. We ourselves don't always know how to fit in. Modern life doesn't really require us to participate in forceful tribal drumming or vision quests. Few men take solitary treks into the wilds to receive their personal spirit-songs. Few know how to construct safe shelters from scratch. Few of us even know how to defend ourselves or our families from harm.

While some of us are comfortable with the image of the modern male, others feel that something has been lost, and that if we're willing to look, we'll be able to see a much vaster vision of manhood. With the waves of change in the latter part of this century, we find ourselves puzzling things we never thought we'd have to puzzle. We live in highly sophisticated surroundings, and are much more secure now than in our primitive past of even a hundred years ago. And yet we are faced with ancient questions of identity.

The role of men and even the idea of manhood is in flux. We confront dangers and life-mysteries no less terrifying than the perils encountered by those who crossed the unknown prairies or explored the uncharted stretches of the Atlantic Ocean. The pressures on us to be effective members of our sex today are as strong as ever— just not so clearly defined.

We are still warriors of one kind or another, called upon to match daring with expertise. Business competition and the search for satisfying, self-affirming jobs can be just as treacherous as navigating through a bay of pirates. The dangers just seem smaller because today's bad guys have more social polish than their earlier counterparts—and better suits.

But this collection is not an ancient battle plan to help us survive the modern mine-fields of our daily lives. It is a forum for the individual voices of men who have faced the same imponderables we have and have something important to say about them. From an Eskimo alone in his kayak out among ice floes to successful movie stars, from philosophers and poets, from the ancient and wise to the young and intuitive come statements born out of intensely reflective moments in their lives—statements that ring true to lawyers and steelworkers, businessmen and warehouse clerks—in short, to all of us. Here is a vision of manhood applicable to all who are willing to look into themselves and into the unknown.

We search the past for images of ourselves as warriors, hunters, lovers, magicians, explorers, and wise men. We question the present and ponder the future for wisdom to guide us. But in the end, perhaps all our questions boil down to the one Bob Dylan asked a few decades ago: How many roads must a man walk down before you call him a man?

Manhood

She felt down into his insides and saw
    bumps and protrusions, how many
cold fenders he'd leaned against, how many
        cold Wyoming nights he'd stood in
as stiff and bristly-haired as those
            far wolves baying at the
farther moon.

Manhood stood tall in tough
levis, taking the wheel in both hands.
Was he meant to steer it down, subdue it to
    docility, take it by the
horns in crisp control? Or navigate
        full-throttle to the stars farther than
thought itself has been
            able to travel, past

plaster busts set in spatial niches in the sky,
    Blake delighted and singing,
        Dante beatifically hook-nosed and sour,
            Oppenheimer sensitive and
apologetic, thought having tried to
        encompass every cubic micro-inch of
black space
and back again, to the
confounding of those card-players sitting at a

four-sided table, knowing no amount of
thought alone can inform everyone there
what's happening atom by atom in the
        universe to start with,
action by action, forward and
        backward in time. . .

Not a word. Manhood so
ruggedly vulnerable. Handsome.

His back is straight.
His gaze is sure.

–Daniel Moore

warrior
wisdom

Boyhood is excitement and disappointment, adventure and misadventure—our first tentative steps out of childhood, greeted with success or our interpretation of failure. We try on various identities. We look into ourselves and up to others in an attempt to determine who we are, or who we want to be.

Young manhood is flexing our muscles a little and experimenting with our newly defined beings in all their raw potential. We're not far removed from the free flight of Peter Pan or the inflated heroism of Superman, and we think we can shoot baskets like Michael Jordan. Later, we may become frustrated when we find we can't fly or dunk.

Most boys and young men lead more or less charmed lives—while some of us, in our hormone-driven roller coaster moods, suffer terribly as youths and spend the rest of our lives trying to undo the psychological knots that were tied too tightly in childhood.

It may be that we need the accumulated muck of messy rooms, male grossness, bathroom jokes, fumbling attempts at romance, and a vigorous fantasy life to make it through these tumultuous years. Whether we're happily conservative, shaggy and hip, or razor-sharp in full rebellion, we need to somehow reach manhood with a feeling that we've arrived. But it's never simple. Somehow we have to cross the borders of inner and outer change into a new territory of growth with a valid passport: a rite of passage that initiates us into the adult male world.

Later, we are both grateful to have left childhood behind and nostalgic for its remembered freedoms. As youths we are directly connected to our own thoughts and emotions. Everything we experience takes place at the center of the universe. And we forever long to have that center back.

But we are still innocent, and we must move from that youthful center to become wise.

A Boy's Summer Song

'Tis fine to play
In the fragrant hay,
And romp on the golden load;
To ride old Jack
To the barn and back,
Or tramp by a shady road.
To pause and drink
At a mossy brink;
Ah, that is the best of joy,
And so I say
On a summer's day,
What's so fine as being a boy?
Ha, Ha!

—Paul Laurence Dunbar

There are children playing in the street who
could solve some of my top problems in
physics . . . they have modes of sensory
perception that I lost long ago.

—J. Robert Oppenheimer

It is the boy who creates the dream; how
could he foresee the man? The man always
fails the boy's dream.

—Leslie Garrett

The Indian world has a deep reverence for solitude and silence. Children are taught at a very early age to sit still and enjoy their solitude in the belief that from this quietude come the most elevated of creative experiences. From this solitude come songs of a special, highly personal nature evolved out of the secret self. Such songs are not shared but are kept strictly to one's self. Dream songs are highly prized by Indians and, like songs of vision, come only to those who search for them.

—Jamake Highwater

Hold childhood in reverence and do not be in any hurry to judge it for good or ill. Give nature time to work before you take over her tasks, lest you interfere with her method.

—Jean Jacques Rousseau

From *Intimations of Immortality*

Behold the Child among his new-born
    blisses,
A six years' Darling of a pygmy size!
See, where 'mid work of his own hand he
    lies,
Fretted by sallies of his mother's kisses,
With light upon him from his father's eyes!
See, at his feet, some little plan or chart,
Some fragment from his dream of human
    life,
Shaped by himself with newly-learnèd art;
    A wedding or a festival,
    A mourning or a funeral;
      And this hath now his heart,
    And unto this he frames his song:
      Then will he fit his tongue
To dialogues of business, love, or strife;
    But it will not be long
    Ere this be thrown aside,
    And with new joy and pride
The little Actor cons another part;
Filling from time to time his "humorous
    stage"
With all the Persons, down to palsied Age,
That Life brings with her in her equipage;
    As if his whole vocation
    Were endless imitation.

                    —William Wordsworth

. . . we want our children to believe that,
inherently, all men are good. But children
know that *they* are not always good; and
often, even when they are, they would prefer
not to be.

–Bruno Bettelheim

Still a child, I admired the hardened convict
upon whom the prison doors are always
closing; I visited the bars and furnished
rooms his stay had consecrated; through *his
eyes* I saw the blue sky and the flowery work
of the countryside; I sniffed out his fatality
through city streets. He had more strength
than a saint, more common sense than a
traveler—and he, he alone! was the sole
witness of his glory and his intelligence.

–Arthur Rimbaud

"Did you have a happy childhood?" is a false
question. As a child I did not know what
happiness was, and whether I was happy or
not. I was too busy *being*.

–Alistair Reid

ADOLESCENCE

Every boy, in his heart, would rather steal
second base than an automobile.

—Tom Clark

Adolescence is a modern invention, a time
before the onset of responsibility. During this
moratorium the not-yet-adult is allowed to
rebel, to play, and to experiment. In
primitive cultures the son was cast in the
same mold as the father. The sacred ways of
the ancestors were repeated without
alteration. Tribal peoples kept their eyes
focused on the past, determined that they
should keep the faith of their fathers, repeat
their virtues, and remain loyal to their
visions of the world.

—Sam Keen

The boy I love, the same becomes a man not
through derived power but in his own
right,
Wicked, rather than virtuous out of
conformity or fear,
Fond of his sweetheart, relishing well his
steak,
Unrequited love or a slight cutting him worse
than a wound cuts,
First rate to ride, to fight, to hit the bull's
eye, to sail a skiff, to sing a song or play
on the banjo,
Preferring scars and faces pitted with
smallpox over all latherers and those
that keep out of the sun.

—Walt Whitman

Children today are tyrants. They contradict
their parents, gobble their food, and
tyrannize their teachers.

—Socrates

The White Horse

The youth walks up to the white horse, to
put its halter on
and the horse looks at him in silence.
They are so silent they are in another world.

—D. H. Lawrence

The evolution of the boy into a birdlike
creature is a natural movement; he looks up
at the light when he wants to escape, as do
birds. Imprisoned birds flutter up the wall
toward any cracks of light. So the young
ascenders often find themselves achieving
spirit, but at the expense of life or their own
grounding in masculine life.

—Robert Bly

Eternal boyhood is the dream of a depressing
percentage of American males, and the
locker room is the temple where they
worship arrested development.

—Russell Baker

You don't have to suffer to be a poet;
adolescence is enough suffering for anyone.

—John Ciardi

When I get involved in something, I just
become consumed by it. When I cut the grass
as a kid, I had to achieve the goal of the best
yard in the neighborhood, and then it was
like, "Okay, I did it."

—Tom Cruise

BEING A SON

I had an amazing vision one time. It had to
do with seeing my whole male lineage
behind my father lined up through a field
and over a hill. It went back hundreds of
generations. I had this tremendous sense that
I was the outcome of all of that work and my
connection to that was very emotional and
very powerful. Not only are you the outcome
of everyone else's previous work of all the
lineages that came before you, but also if you
perfect yourself and cleanse yourself and get
rid of all the guilt and all the suffering, then
you get rid of it for all those who came
before you, too. As you free yourself, you
free the whole horde. I felt that I was one
with all this *love* from all these *men*
before me.

—Richard Gere

When I was a boy of fourteen, my father was so ignorant I could hardly stand to have the old man around. But when I got to be twenty-one, I was astonished at how much he had learned in seven years.

—Mark Twain

. . . what the child is doing in the inside of his mother's body is scooping it out; "this desire to suck and scoop out, first directed to her breast, soon extends to the inside of her body." Excavation. The child is hollowing out a cave for himself inside his mother's body. We are still unborn; we are still in a cave; Plato's cave. "Behold, men live in a sort of cavernous underground chamber, with a long passage stretching towards the light all down the cave. Here they have lived from childhood, chained by the leg and by the neck, so that they cannot move and can look only straight forwards, the chains preventing them from turning their heads. At some distance higher up there is the light of a fire burning behind them; and between the fire and the prisoners there is a raised track, with a parapet built along it, like the screen at a puppet show, which hides the men who work the puppets."

—Norman O. Brown

To become a man, a son must first become a prodigal, leave home, and travel solo into a far country. Alien nation before reconciliation. There can be no homecoming without leavetaking. To love a woman we must first leave WOMAN behind.

—Sam Keen

The children despise their parents until the age of forty, when they suddenly become just like them—thus preserving the system.

—Quentin Crewe

It's a wonderful thing when your father becomes not a god but a man to you—when he comes down from the mountain and you see he's this man with weaknesses. And you love him as this whole being, not as a figurehead.

—Robin Williams

Like Father Like Son

The failure of my father's mind at eighty-six
adds itself to the wheel of sorrow almost
    gently.
If only it brought some brute peace in its
    wake
instead of these half-formed hatreds and
    suspicions.

I drive the coast road where a solid wave of
    faces
hack wings from vertical rocks and hawks
    whistle
across the edge on a wrong-sided knife.

That night I awaken suddenly, crying out!

—Michael Hannon

My father died three days ago. I walked
onstage the other night in front of all those
people and felt like I had to celebrate him. It
was like a wake for me, so it was kind of
joyous. Why do we perform? One of the
reasons I became a performer was to get
attention from my parents. So the ultimate
kind of attention you can get is to become a
celebrity. Your parents *have* to take notice of
you at that point.

—Sting

RITES OF PASSAGE

The most important and sweeping function of a primitive initiation was to provide a youth with a sense of his own personal significance within the context of a greater world. In becoming a man he took his place alongside his fathers and forefathers; by discovering his tribal heritage he became connected with the ongoing flow of life. He was transformed into a spiritual being as he joined his ancestors in a universal brotherhood that cut through time.

–Ray Raphael

When I was a kid in the '40s, discipline began at home. But there's a different type of kid now whose rite of passage is a 9-millimeter pistol and a vial of crack.

–Robert L. Jones

In a strange way, fear is the only guide to be completely trusted. The next step seems always to come out of a place of darkness, out of the tension of not knowing. The crux of "What now?" lies in your own experience, in containing the apprehension of uncertainty and being willing not to know and not to be told.

—Wayne Liebman

From *A Shaman's Initiation*

When I was a young man I used to dream all sorts of insignificant things just like any other man. But once, I saw myself going down a road until I reached a tree. With an axe in my hand, I went round the tree and wanted to fell it. Then I heard a voice saying: "Later!" and I woke up.

Next day the neighbors said to me: "Go and fell a tree for the *kuojka* sledge!" I set out, found a suitable tree and started to cut it down. When the tree fell, a man sprang out of its roots with a loud shout. I was petrified with fear.

The man asked, "Where are you going?"

"I am going to my tent."

"Why, of course, since you have a tent, you must go there. Well, my friend, I am a man, who came out of the roots of the tree. The root is thick, it looks thin in your eyes only. Therefore I tell you that you must come down through the root if you wish to see me."

"What sort of tree is that?" I asked. "I never could find it out."

The man answered: "From times of old, it is of this tree that the *kuojka* sledges have been made and the shamans have been growing from. Rocked in the cradle, they become shamans—well that's what this tree is for."

"All right, I shall go with you."

—Sereptie

Happy is he who, having seen these rites, goes below the hollow earth; for he knows the end of life and he knows its god-sent beginning.

—Pindar

W

hen do we become men? What is it that defines that forward progression from adolescence to manhood? Is it the car? Have we been to college? Do we have the foggiest idea what we want to be doing for the rest of our lives?

Because time tends to appear nowadays in fast-cutting MTV-esque edits, with commercial breaks, our sense of continuity may get jumbled. We were just over there doing one thing, now we find ourselves over here doing—maybe even **being**—something totally different. One moment we're going to school, the next moment we're behind a desk, or married with children.

Many of us scratch our heads and wonder how we got here.

Suddenly we have responsibilities. There are

expectations of us in the bedroom and in the home, in the workplace, and in front of the automatic teller. Some find themselves adrift in these new waters, as if there had never been an effective model man in their lives to teach them the basics of how to cope. Others carry these new expectations with apparent ease; there is no break in the link between these men and the men before them—you can sense it in their bearing.

Most men face the howling winds of life with a more or less positive sense of self. Even with nameless fears and low self-esteem, with pent-up angers and the edgy grouchiness that comes from being fresh out of boyhood, most of us are able to function with some nobility from day to day.

At the end of it all, manhood is not so much a definition as a way of being. The obsessive concern about what manhood **is** can block the free flow of life that surges through all of us. Narcissus died looking at his own reflection, until the rest of the world entirely disappeared.

A man might find his true definition emerging when he says, "I can't be defined!" or when he proclaims like Whitman, "Do I contradict myself? Very well, I contradict myself. I contain multitudes!"

The cosmos is a great man, and man is a little cosmos.

—Sufi saying

A man's usefulness depends upon his living up to his ideals insofar as he can. It is hard to fail but it is worse never to have tried to succeed. All daring and courage, all iron endurance of misfortune, make for a finer, nobler type of manhood. Only those are fit to live who do not fear to die, and none are fit to die who have shrunk from the joy of the life and the duty of life.

—Theodore Roosevelt

Everybody wants to *be* somebody; nobody wants to *grow*.

—Wolfgang von Goethe

Man with wooden leg escapes prison. He's caught. They take his wooden leg away from him. Each day he must cross a large hill and swim a wide river to get to the field where he must work all day on one leg. This goes on for a year. At the Christmas Party they give him back his leg. Now he doesn't want it. His escape is all planned. It requires only one leg.

—James Tate

In the present crisis in masculinity we do not need, as some feminists are saying, *less* masculine power. We need more Man psychology. We need to develop a sense of calmness about masculine power so we don't have to act out dominating, disempowering behavior toward others.

—Robert Moore and Douglas Gilette

You cannot run away from a weakness; you must sometime fight it out or perish. And if that be so, why not now, and where you stand?

—Robert Louis Stevenson

Women do not like timid men. Cats do not like prudent mice.

—H. L. Mencken

When you follow a team intimately, year after year, the passage of time slows to a benign crawl, and the difference between youth and middle age becomes inextricable.

—Michael Bamberger

All that I know I learned after I was thirty.

—Georges Clemenceau

From *Walking Around*

It just so happens I'm tired of being a man.

It just so happens I go into tailorshops and
  movie theatres

faded and impenetrable, like a swan made of
  felt

crossing a water of origins and ashes.

The smell of barbershops makes me bawl
  like a baby.

I just want a time-out of stones or wool,

I just don't want to see establishments or
  gardens,

merchandise, eyeglasses, or elevators.

It just so happens I'm tired of my feet and
  my fingernails

and my hair and my shadow.

It just so happens I'm tired of being a man.

—Pablo Neruda

Men vent great passions by breaking into
song, as we observe in the most grief-stricken
and the most joyful.

—Giambattista Vico

What can we do? We were born with the
Great Unrest. Our father taught us that life is
one long journey on which only the unfit are
left behind.

—Caribou Eskimo to Dr. Knud Rassmussen

Modern men, anxious as we are, uncertain of
ourselves, lost without a map, may be better
equipped to survive than our more solid and
unquestioning forebears. Paradoxically, our
instability may be the key to our strength.

—Sam Keen

. . . Man has a small furnace in his abdomen.
It is called the Tan Tien (pronounced don-
CHEN), and a man uses it to burn his
sufferings. The idea is not that by doing so he
gets rid of his pain, but that he turns his pain
to fuel which makes him stronger.

—Wayne Liebman

What's the actual identity, what's the actual inner person, *is* there even an inner self, is there any identity? Anybody's identity problem is the entire universe, it's as vast as the entire universe.

−Allen Ginsberg

One of the pleasures of middle age is to find out that one *was* right, and that one was much righter than one knew at, say, seventeen or twenty-three.

−Ezra Pound

One wouldn't want to love oneself. That damages our usefulness. One wouldn't want to pursue the past. That is bad for the posture. And one wouldn't want to be one of those old men who take out their cocks and clear their throats as if they were about to write, with their seminal discharge, one of those lengthy postwar treaties that will crush the national spirit, surrender the critical isthmus, and yield the mountain passes to the enemy.

−John Cheever

When you're betting for tiles in an archery
contest, you shoot with skill. When you're
betting for fancy belt buckles, you worry
about your aim. And when you're betting for
real gold, you're a nervous wreck. Your skill
is the same in all three cases—but because
one prize means more to you than another,
you let outside considerations weigh on your
mind. He who looks too hard at the outside
gets clumsy on the inside.

—Chuang Chou

In the middle of the road of our life
I found myself in a dark wood
Whose straight way was lost—
Ah, how to say how heavy a thing
This wild, rough and powerful wood was to
     me—
Just to think of it brings on the fear again!

—Dante Alighieri

A hero in a movie should never cry in the
presence of his wife or child.

—John Wayne

43

I was crying," said Dean.
"Ah hell, you never cry."
"You say that? Why do you think I don't cry?"
"You don't die enough to cry."

–Jack Kerouac

By Him in whose hand my soul is, if you
knew what I know you would weep much
and laugh little.

–The Prophet Muhammad

A man would not hesitate to spend
      everything he had—if he only knew the
      secret of his own heart.
If a man could grasp the bliss of his secret he
      would shed a tear with every breath he
      breathed.

–Shaykh Muhammad ibn al-Habib

My God, I am so emotional that sometimes I
can't stand the intensity. Oh, my God. Then
they ask me if I ever cry? I say, "Holy shit,
probably two days ago." I'm very subject to
violent fits of weeping, for very good
reasons.

–William S. Burroughs

For a Tear is an Intellectual Thing,
And a Sigh is the Sword of an Angel King,
And the bitter groan of the Martyr's woe
Is an Arrow from the Almightie's Bow.

–William Blake

BEING A HUSBAND

Keep your eyes wide open before marriage, half shut afterwards.

—Benjamin Franklin

When a man marries he has fulfilled half of his religion—so let him fear God concerning the other half!

—The Prophet Muhammad

The great secret of successful marriage is to treat all disasters as incidents and none of the incidents as disasters.

—Harold Nicholson

I have a wife, you have a wife, we all have
wives, we've had a taste of paradise, we
know what it means to be married.

—Sholem Aleichem

The Way
My love's manners in bed
are not to be discussed by me,
as mine by her
I would not credit comment upon gracefully.

Yet I ride by the margin of that lake in
the wood, the castle,
and the excitement of strongholds,
and have a small boy's notion of doing good.

Oh well, I will say here,
knowing each man,
let you find a good wife too,
and love her as hard as you can.

—Robert Creeley

So ought men to love their wives as their
own bodies. He that loveth his wife loveth
himself.

For no man ever yet hated his own
flesh; but nourisheth and cherisheth it, even
as the Lord the church:

For we are members of his body, of
his flesh, and of his bones.

For this cause shall a man leave his
father and mother, and shall be joined unto
his wife, and they two shall be one flesh.

–Ephesians 5:28-33

When a Man has Married a Wife
    he finds out whether
Her Knees & elbows are only
        glued together

–William Blake

Marriage is a feast where the grace is
sometimes better than the dinner.

–Charles Caleb Colton

Deceive not thyself by overexpecting
happiness in the married estate. Remember
the nightingales which sing only some
months in the spring, but commonly are
silent when they have hatched their eggs.

–Thomas Fuller

Husbands never become good; they merely become proficient.

—H. L. Mencken

Love has to be reinvented, we know that. The only thing women can hope for is security. Once they get that, heart and beauty go out the window. All they have left is cold disdain, the food of most marriages nowadays.

—Arthur Rimbaud

We master women by exuding a male knowableness. Men yuk about women being mysterious, but it's usually the other way around. Women lay themselves open to men who stay silent: many, many women build their lives around their men, derive their identity from them. They often sacrifice their friendship with other women in doing so, while the men hide large patches of their lives and living processes. Such an imbalance gives men great power over women, and we use it.

—Nicholas von Hoffman

Should I get married? Should I be good?
Astound the girl next door with my velvet
   suit and faustus hood?

–Gregory Corso

You can bear your own Faults, and why not
a Fault in your Wife.

–Benjamin Franklin

BEING A FATHER

Changing Diapers
How intelligent he looks!
   on his back
   both feet caught in my one hand
   his glance set sideways,
   on a giant poster of Geronimo
   with a Sharp's repeating rifle by his knee.

I open, wipe, he doesn't even notice
   nor do I.
Baby legs and knees
   toes like little peas
   little wrinkles, good-to-eat,
   eyes bright, shiny ears,
   chest swelling drawing air,

No trouble, friend,
   you and me and Geronimo
   are men.

                    –Gary Snyder

I find myself leaning more toward light
comedy now because I have a 2 year-old son.
I don't really want to come home every day
thinking about the Vietnamese girl who was
raped, murdered and thrown off the bridge.
It makes it tough to play with my son. I don't
have aspirations to change the world, just to
make a nice, simple movie.

–Michael J. Fox

Fathers should be neither seen nor heard.
That is the only proper basis for family life.

–Oscar Wilde

Never raise your hand to your children; it
leaves your midsection unprotected.

–Robert Orben

To His Son

Three things there be that prosper all apace
And flourish, while they are asunder far;
But on a day they meet all in a place,
And when they meet, they one another mar.
And they be these: the wood, the weed, the
    wag.
The wood is that that makes the gallows tree;
The weed is that that strings the hangman's
    bag;
The wag, my pretty knave, betokens thee.
Now mark, dear boy: while these assemble
    not,
Green springs the tree, hemp grows, the wag
    is wild;
But when they meet, it makes the timber rot,
It frets the halter, and it chokes the child.
    God bless the child!

–Sir Walter Raleigh

The first half of our life is ruined by our
parents and the second half by our children.

–Clarence Darrow

When they were four or five we would go
over to Bald Mountain on foot and we could
look back and see our place. When they were
seven and eight, we went up to Grouse Ridge
on foot and we could look down from Grouse
Ridge to see Bald Mountain from which you
can see our place. A few years later we went
on up to the High Sierra and got up on 8,000
foot English Mountain from which you can
see Grouse Ridge. And then we went on over
to Castle Peak which is the highest peak in
that range which is 10,000 feet high and
climbed that and you can see English
Mountain from there. Then we went on
north and we climbed Sierra Buttes and
Mount Lassen—Mount Lassen is the farthest
we've been out now. So from Mount Lassen,
you can see Castle Peak, you can see English
Peak, you can see Grouse Ridge, you can see
Bald Mountain and you can see our place.
That is the way the world should be learned.
It's an intense geography that is never far
removed from your body.

—Gary Snyder

BEING A FRIEND

The bonds of friendship are not inseparable
Those who haven't any friends and want
    some are often creepy
Those who have friends and don't want them
    are doomed
Those who haven't any friends and don't
    want any are grand
Those who have friends and want them seem
    sadly human

—Gregory Corso

Neither love nor hate forever. Treat your
friends as though they could become your
worst enemies. Since this happens in reality,
let it happen in foresight. We shouldn't give
arms to the turncoats of friendship; they will
wage the worst sort of war with them. On
the contrary, when it comes to enemies,
leave the door open to reconciliation.

—Baltasar Gracián

Men do not criticize those who conform.
This is what it means to enjoy comradeship
with men.

— Chuang Chou

I have perceived that to be with those I like
    is enough,
To stop in company with the rest at evening
    is enough,
To be surrounded by beautiful curious
    breathing laughing flesh is enough,
To pass among them . . . to touch any one . . .
    to rest my arm ever so lightly round his
    or her neck for a moment . . . what is
    this then?
I do not ask any more delight . . . I swim in it
    as in a sea.

— Walt Whitman

. . . your tongue should not mention a
brother's faults either in his absence or his
presence. Instead, you should always pretend
ignorance. You should not contradict him
when he talks, nor dispute or argue with
him. Do not pry into his affairs, nor quiz him
about things he wishes to keep secret.
    . . . Keep silent about the secrets he
does confide in you, and never tell them to a
third person—not even to one of his closest

friends. Do not reveal anything about a brother at all to anyone, not even after you have broken off from him, for that would show a meanness of your character and an impurity of your innermost heart.

—al-Ghazali

Let all Men know thee, but no man know thee thoroughly: Men freely ford that see the shallows.

—Benjamin Franklin

Fraternity comes into being after the sons are expelled from the family; when they form their own club, in the wilderness, away from home, away from women. The brotherhood is a substitute family, a substitute woman—alma mater.

—Norman O. Brown

The bird a nest, the spider a web, man
friendship.

—William Blake

F ated to be male by a genetic fork in the road (the Y chromosome that differentiates the male body from the female body with its double Xs), our bodies are both physically and metaphysically very different from women's. Flat where a woman's body is round, extrovertedly protruding, a male body bounds from the diving board of physicality—free of bearing children and fit for a different kind of physiological flight.

This body of ours is both ancient and new. It develops much as it has for centuries—it is a body well-formed to climb sheer rockfaces, stand in feverish jungle mud and fire at invisible guerrillas. And yet it is a new body—we live in it here and now. We experience everything through it, measuring both ourselves and the world by its sensorial yardstick.

From muscle-bound hulks to ectomorphic eggheads, all men share the same basic characteristics and the biological mythology that goes with them. Our male bodies today may have fewer obstacles to conquer in our plush business offices (except for the occasional struggle to conquer the squash courts), but the mythology endures.

And, of course, as bearers of seed, lovers, husbands, and fathers, our male conduit transmits the physical bodies of future generations that carry forward the original light of the human species, male and female. We are not merely good swimmers with wiggling tails and a cunning sense of direction—we are the igniters of physical creation in the womb.

Dance Russe

If when my wife is sleeping
and the baby and Kathleen
are sleeping
and the sun is a flame-white disc
in silken mists
above shining trees,—
if I in my north room
dance naked, grotesquely
before my mirror
waving my shirt round my head
and singing softly to myself:
"I am lonely, lonely.
I was born to be lonely,
I am best so!"
If I admire my arms, my face,
my shoulders, flanks, buttocks
against the yellow drawn shades,—

Who shall say I am not
the happy genius of my household?

—William Carlos Williams

A Woman Scaly & a Man all Hairy
Is such a Match as he who dares
Will find the Woman's Scales scrape off the
    Man's Hairs.

—William Blake

The body is the organism in which motion
makes visible the sacred forms of life itself.

—Jamake Highwater

An intact body image is an essential
prerequisite for a full understanding of the
shape of the world. . . . The most inescapable
experience we have is the sensation of our
bodily self, and it is only in the course of
growing up and acquiring skilled movements
that we learn to tell the difference between
the part of the world that is us and the part
that is outside us.

—Jonathan Miller

An attitude of the body can embody a whole
world view.

—David Byrne

Denied hungers of the physical-gene-body
are contradictions of spirit. Hungers for sex,
food, loveliness, and love are manifestations
of the spirit who is a manbeast.

—Michael McClure

On earth, man is weighed down by gravity,
his body encased in heavy muscles; he
sweats; he runs; he strikes; even, with
difficulty, he leaps. At times, nevertheless, I
have unmistakably seen, amidst the darkness
of fatigue, the first tinges of color that herald
what I have called the dawn of the flesh.

—Yukio Mishima

My muscular agility has always been greatest
when my creative power has flowed most
abundantly. The *body* is inspired: let us leave
the "soul" out of it.

—Friedrich Nietzsche

Shun asked his teacher, Ch'eng, "Is it
possible to possess God?"

"Even your body is not yours, so how
could you possess God?"

"Well, if it isn't mine, whose is it?"

"It's a shape that nature has given
you. Your birth is not yours either; it's a
harmony conferred by nature. Your life is
not yours; it's an acquiescence conferred by
nature. Your grandsons and sons are not
yours; they are a slough conferred by nature.
That is why you travel, but do not know

where you are going. You abide, but you do
not know what is holding you up. You eat
without knowing what you are tasting. All
this is the strong, Yang breath of nature in
action. How could you possess that?"

—Chuang Chou

The expression of a wellmade man appears
    not only in his face,
It is in his limbs and joints also . . . it is
    curiously in the joints of his hips and
    wrists,
It is in his walk . . . the carriage of his neck
    . . . the flex of his waist and knees . . .
    dress does not hide him,
The strong sweet supple quality he has
    strikes through the cotton and flannel;
To see him pass conveys as much as the best
    poem . . . perhaps more,
You linger to see his back and the back of his
    neck and shoulderside.

—Walt Whitman

SEXUALITY

I hate to give away secrets, but I did have a
very effective opening line. It's very simple.
Since I traveled the world so much,
especially throughout America, I knew my
geography. I'd always ask, "Where are you
from?" And when she would answer, I'd
pretend that I was from some small place
close to it, and we would immediately be on
common ground. She might say, "I'm from
Portland, Oregon." And I would say, "No
kidding? I was born in Lake Oswego." She
wouldn't believe me, but then I'd say, "How
could I make that up?" And she'd say,
"You're right." That approach has worked for
me all over the world.

–Wilt Chamberlain

The big difference between sex for money
and sex for free is that sex for money usually
costs a lot less.

—Brendan Behan

I have always, beyond belief, hoped to meet,
at night and in a woods, a beautiful naked
woman or rather, since such a wish once
expressed means nothing, I regret, beyond
belief, not having met her.

—André Breton

As we live, we are transmitters of life.
And when we fail to transmit life, life fails to
flow through us.

—D. H. Lawrence

The possession of the perfect penis has been
the dream of many mortal men. It is the
physical evidence of their ability as lovers
and the key to earning respect and
admiration not only from their female sexual
partners but also from their male
competitors. A primitive attitude it may be,
but the penis will always remain an innate
feature of maleness.

—Kennith Purvis, M.D.

The unspoken meaning is always sexual. Of sexuality we can have only symbolical knowledge, because sexual is carnal. Death and love are altogether carnal; hence their great magic and their great terror. . . . It is the fool King Lear who asks his daughters to tell how much they love him. And it is the one who loves him who is silent.

—Norman O. Brown

Come to think of it, there is nothing more metaphysical and spiritual than the symbolism of sexuality.

—Alan Watts

I am more attracted by beautiful details—the mouth, the nose—than by the whole. Finding myself in front of a beauty can be frightening. A beautiful woman whom you love is always a danger for you. You are always afraid that someone will take her away from you. I much prefer a non-beauty with a great personality.

—Giorgio Armani

From *The Mahanirvana Tantra*

He should then with his wife get on the bed,
and there sit with his face towards the East
or the North. Then, looking at his wife, let
him embrace her with his left arm, and,
placing his right hand over her head, let him
intone the *mantras* appropriate to the
different parts of her body: over her head the
mantra *"Klim"* a hundred times; over her chin
"A-im" a hundred times; over her throat
"Shrim" twenty times, and the same a
hundred times over each of her two breasts.
He should then intone *"Hrim"* ten times over
her heart, and twenty-five times over her
navel. Next, let him place his hand on her
vagina and intone *"Klim A-im"* a
hundred-and-eight times (equals the number
of beads on a rosary), and then the same over
his own member. And then, intoning *"Hrim"*
let him open her vagina, and let him go into
her to beget a child. The husband should, at
the time of the spending of his seed, be
aware of this event as *brahman*, reality itself,
discharging it deeply into her womb, and at
the same time intone:

> *Yathagnina sagarbha bhur, daur, yatha*
> *Vajra-dharina,*
> *Vayuna dig garbha-vati, tatha garbha-vati*
> *bhava.*

(As the earth is pregnant of fire and
        heaven of Indra,
As space is pregnant of air, so do thou
        also become pregnant.)
                    —7th-century East Indian religious text

To give pleasure was to exaggerate the
already absolute separation between lives.
You intruded your hand between the legs of
another person only to feel more heatedly
than ever the demarcation of your skins. . . .
        Everyone is alone, thought Martin,
and everyone is the same.
                                    —Jesse Green

Morality in sexual relations, when it is free
from superstition, consists essentially of
respect for the other person, and
unwillingness to use that person solely as a
means of personal gratification, without
regard to his or her desires.
                                    —Bertrand Russell

Power is the ultimate aphrodisiac.

                                    —Henry Kissinger

Money, it turned out, was exactly like sex.
You thought of nothing else if you didn't
have it, and thought of other things if you
did.

                                    —James Baldwin

I believe in sex and death—two experiences
that come once in a lifetime.

                                    —Woody Allen

The great Scottish-American naturalist John Muir (1838-1914) once said, "The clearest way into the universe is through a forest wilderness." Few of us have lived in, or even near, a forest. But whenever we sample even the smallest taste of the wild—and sense our own wildness connecting with it—we feel deeply at home.

A great sunset and a walk by a rushing stream can go straight to our hearts. A breath of fresh air from a mountaintop, with that raw scent of pine, lifts us out of our day-to-day lives. It expands our individual identities for a moment—and takes us into somewhere timeless.

Men usually experience the wild by butting up against it. We pit ourselves against the elements through hunting, building, and exploration. But as late twentieth-century men, many of us feel an acute need to get in touch with the wilderness again. We want to tap into the wild that exists both without and within us, perhaps as a way to offset the air-conditioned comforts of modern life, or the hectic stresses of the big cities that have dulled our senses and our minds.

Although we cannot easily go back to the golden, naturally heroic times of the "noble savage," there are ways in which we can connect to a cosmic wildness in our lives without running naked through the streets.

We can purify our senses. If we take notice of the natural ebbs and flows of energy within us and revel in the visible play of the elements outside us, we can renew ourselves. We must be open enough to set out on unmarked paths—in nature and in our own masculine wildness—to fulfill the haunting call that echoes up through our beings as men.

Break with the outside world, live like a
bear.

–Gustave Flaubert

I never saw a wild thing
Sorry for itself.

–D. H. Lawrence

Our bodies are wild. The involuntary quick
turn of the head at a shout, the vertigo at
looking off a precipice, the heart-in-the-throat
in a moment of danger, the catch of the
breath, the quiet moments relaxing, staring,
reflecting—are universal responses of the
mammal body. . . . The body does not
require the intercession of some conscious
intellect to make it breathe, to keep the heart
beating . . . it is a life of its own. . . . The
body is, so to speak, in the mind. They are
both wild.

–Gary Snyder

Every normal man must be tempted at times
to spit on his hands, hoist the black flag, and
begin slitting throats.

–H. L. Mencken

There are times when I'm running on the
beach and I feel primordial, ancient. And
then there are times when I feel like a
brand-new cell, just formed.

—Nicholas Cage

Eventually, all things merge into one, and a
river runs through it. The river was cut by
the world's great flood and runs over rocks
from the basement of time. On some of the
rocks are timeless raindrops. Under the rocks
are the words, and some of the words are
theirs.

I am haunted by waters.

—Norman MacLean

My grandfather always said that living is like
licking honey off a thorn.

—Louis Adamic

Climb the mountains and get their good tidings. Nature's peace will flow into you as sunshine flows into trees. The winds will blow their own freshness into you, and the storms their energy, while cares will drop off like autumn leaves.

–John Muir

At the same time that we are earnest to explore and learn all things, we require that all things be mysterious and unexplorable, that land and sea be infinitely wild, unsurveyed and unfathomed by us because unfathomable. We can never have enough of Nature.

–Henry David Thoreau

What would life be if we had no courage to attempt anything?

–Vincent van Gogh

The dangerous aspects of nature that kept
our forebears watchful and humble have
now almost disappeared outside; but they
have turned inward (wilderness
without—wilderness within!) so that the
whole of Western society rapidly approaches
the physical and mental cracking point from
the inner dangers alone. This is no joking
matter, for should the outer wilderness
disappear altogether, it would inevitably
resurrect powerfully from within,
whereupon it would immediately be
projected. Enemies would be created, and its
terrifying aspects would take revenge for our
neglect, our lack of reverence, our ruthless
interference with that beautiful order of
things.

—C. A. Meier

The fragmented consciousness is intense.
The possessor burns brightly. When man is
alone he is on fire. When man is Love he is
on fire. When man sleeps he is a
constellation. *Alert in the forest at night.*

—Michael McClure

I woke up in the middle of the night and climbed out of the tent to make coffee. There was no sound save the wind and, in all that space, not one light, just a scant new moon that hung in the sky like a fine silk thread. The twentieth century had vanished. I raised my cup in a toast. As always after days spent in Big Bend, I felt only two kinds of time: never and forever.

—Richard West

Hope is a word like a snowdrift—This is the Great Knowing, this is the Awakening, this is Voidness—So shut up, live, travel, adventure, bless and don't be sorry.

—Jack Kerouac

I'll come back with iron limbs, dark skin and furious eyes; in this guise they will think I've descended from a strong race. I will have gold; I will be indolent and brutal. Women nurse these ferocious invalids come home from the hot countries.

—Arthur Rimbaud

There are many fine things about Nature, but
it does no talking.

—Chuang Chou

A Bull in a China Shop
I'm a bull in a china shop,
when it comes to clear thinking;
I'm a bull in a china shop,
when it comes to being aware:
first, I make a fiery snort,
then shake my enormous horns . . .
I shoot lightning from my eyes,
& become a thunderstorm.

I'm a bull in a china shop,
when it comes to understanding;
I'm a bull in a china shop,
in matters of the heart:
delicate teacups, dainty saucers,
& fragile knick-knacks
go flying every-which-way,
& fall to the floor with a crash.

—Harvey Taylor

We are in the minority in the great realm of being, and with a genius for adjustment, we frequently seek to join the multitudes. We are in the minority within our own nature, and in the agony and battle of passions we often choose to envy the beast. We behave as if the animal kingdom were our lost paradise, to which we are trying to return for moments of delight, believing that it is the animal state in which happiness consists.

—Abraham Joshua Heschel

I think of myself as a young prince from a long line of royalty. My sign is Leo. A Leo has to walk with pride. When he takes a step, he has to put his foot down. You walk into a room and you want people to know your presence, without you doing anything. I think I have kind of a natural magnetism. I don't see myself as extremely handsome. I just figure I can charm you into liking me.

—Wesley Snipes

If I worship any particular thing it shall be
    some of the spread of my body;
Translucent mould of me it shall be you,
Shaded ledges and rests, firm masculine
    coulter, it shall be you,
Whatever goes to the tilth of me it shall be
    you,
You my rich blood, your milky stream pale
    strippings of my life;
Breast that presses against other breasts it
    shall be you,
My brain it shall be your occult convolutions,
Root of washed sweet-flag, timorous
    pond-snipe, nest of guarded duplicate
    eggs, it shall be you,
Mixed tussled hay of head and beard and
    brawn it shall be you,
Trickling sap of maple, fibre of manly wheat,
    it shall be you;
Sun so generous it shall be you,
Vapors lighting and shading my face it shall
    be you,
You sweaty brooks and dews it shall be you,
Winds whose soft-tickling genitals rub
    against me it shall be you,
Broad muscular fields, branches of liveoak,
    living lounger in my winding paths, it
    shall be you,
Hands I have taken, face I have kissed,
    mortal I have ever touched, it shall be
    you.

                        –Walt Whitman

Abbot Moses said: A man who lives apart
from other men is like a ripe grape. And a
man who lives in the company of others is a
sour grape.

-Sayings from the Desert Fathers of the Fourth Century

What a thing it is to sit absolutely alone in
the forest at night, cherished by this
wonderful, unintelligent perfectly innocent
speech, the most comforting speech in the
world. . . . Nobody started it, nobody is going
to stop it. It will talk as long as it wants, the
rain. As long as it talks I am going to listen.

-Thomas Merton

I didn't need a house then, or a pasture.
Somewhere there would be a cave, a crack in
the rocks, where I could hole up during a
rain. I wanted the plants and the stones to
tell me their secrets. I talked to them. I
roamed. I was like a part of the earth.
Everything had been taken from me except
myself. Now and then, in some place or
other, I looked at my face in a mirror to
remind myself who I was.

-John (Fire) Lame Deer

He who mounts a wild elephant goes where
the wild elephant goes.

—Randolph Bourne

Once upon a time in America, a man's character was formed by hard work, or so the mythology goes—around the farm before sunup, or on the streets of New York, selling newspapers. Hard work made the boy tough, and the man deep. Character back then came from traditions which today are hard to come by. If a man's character is formed by today's television portrayals of forbearance, honesty, sincerity and the like, God help us!

And yet, fine elements of character are still present among us. If character is showing compassion to the afflicted, proving ourselves courageous in a crisis, or being even-tempered and dependable, then great instances of character are retold daily in the media.

The great puzzle facing us today is how to learn these noble character traits ourselves—and how to pass those traits on to our children. With masculine attributes such as aggression, patriotism, and self-interest under siege in modern society, it is difficult to know where to turn for exemplary models of good character.

But perhaps these difficulties are not new. We've always been hard nuts to crack—every man born on earth has had to unearth the golden treasure of his noble character. As Confucius said around 300 B.C., "In general, man's heart and mind are a greater obstacle than mountains and streams; they present more difficulties than understanding nature."

Who can understand
the hearts of the truly great,
which are harder than diamonds
and softer than flowers?

—Bhavabhuti

Be in the world as though you were a
stranger or a wayfarer, and consider yourself
one of the inhabitants of the graves.

—The Prophet Muhammad

Search others for their virtues, thyself for thy
vices.

—Benjamin Franklin

Do everything. One thing may turn out right.

—Humphrey Bogart

Behavior influences consciousness. Right
behavior means right consciousness. Our
attitude here and now influences the entire
environment: our words, actions, ways of
holding and moving ourselves, they all
influence what happens around us and inside
us. The actions of every instant, every day,
must be right. . . . Every gesture is important.
How we eat, how we put on our clothes,
how we wash ourselves, how we go to the
toilet, how we put our things away, how we
act with other people, family, wife, work.
How we are—totally—in every single gesture.

—Taisen Deshimaru

The one who flatters his own or someone
else's ego will never smell the perfume of
sincerity.

—Abu 'Abdullah al-Qurashi

Only he will deserve the name of man and
can count upon anything prepared for him
from Above, who has already acquired
corresponding data for being able to preserve
intact both the wolf and the sheep confided
to his care.

—G. I. Gurdjieff

I didn't make myself, and you didn't make yourself. I didn't do all those things myself. It was done for me. We don't choose to draw air into our own lungs. God does it for us. He's usin' me for a vessel.

–Muhammad Ali

Do not despair of life. Think of the fox, prowling in a winter night to satisfy his hunger. His race survives; I do not believe any of them ever committed suicide.

–Henry David Thoreau

Utitiaq's Song

Aja, I am joyful—this is good!

Aja, nothing but ice all around me, that is good!

Aja, I am joyful—this is good!

My homeland is nothing but slush, that is good!

Aja, I am joyful—this is good!

Aja, Oh when will this end? This is good!

I am tired of watching and waking—this is good!

–Cumberland Sound Eskimo
[after being adrift on the ice for a week]

Romantic melancholy is the feeling that the
world isn't quite up to your demands on it,
and classical melancholy is the feeling that
you're not quite up to the world's demands
on you.

—Adam Gopnik

Good impulses spring from a happy
readiness of spirit. For such a spirit there are
no tight spots, no troubling chance
occurrences, only vivacity and brio. Some
think much, and then do everything wrong,
and others get everything right without any
forethought at all.

—Baltasar Gracián

I always want the upper hand. If you do
something repeatedly, you lose a little bit of
hunger each time. It's up to you to push
yourself to regain that hunger.

—Michael Jordan

When a man has boils or scabies, he isn't disgusted with himself; he puts his infected hand in his dish and he licks his fingers without any repugnance. But if he sees a small sore on someone else's hand, he can't swallow his food. It's the same with moral blemishes: when you see defects such as indifference, pride, and lust in yourself, they don't bother you; but as soon as you notice them in others, you feel hurt and resentful.

—Jalaluddin Rumi

The older you are, the more you have an unconscious drive to try to act according to your convictions. I think that people, whether they know it or not, always want more integrity in their life—literally, a more integrated life, where your mind and your body and your spirit are all in the same place at the same time.

—Bill Clinton

To me, what makes Malcolm [X] *Malcolm* is
not the rhetoric, not the fiery summons to
battle, it's not even the call that blacks
resume their manhood by any means
necessary. NO. It is study, reading. Malcolm
learned to understand the Man and the
system that was his enemy. Having learned
what racism was, he was wise enough to
come up with a strategy for black survival.
This was a man who remained a student all
his life.

—Ossie Davis

Always have the situation under control,
even if losing. Never betray an inward sense
of defeat.

—Arthur Ashe

Confucius: In the case of nature, we still
have such tangibles as the four seasons,
dawn, and evening, but man is rich in
appearances and deep in realities. That is
why some look all right, but are really
addicts. Some are fully matured, but look
degenerate. Others are timid, but
understanding. Some look firm, but are lax;
others look relaxed, but are ardent. That is

why some approach propriety as though they were thirsty, but then stop being polite as though it were something hot. Therefore, when he sends men on missions, the prince is observing them for loyalty. When he uses them near home, he is observing them for respectfulness. When he importunes them, he is observing them for ability. When he puts unexpected questions to them, he is observing them for knowledge. When he sets an early date for accomplishment, he is observing their devotion to duty. When he charges them with appropriations, he is observing how closely they achieve the human ideal. When he informs them of the dangers ahead, he is observing them for morality. When he gets them drunk with wine, he is observing them for depravity. When he has them live in a large variety of places, he is observing them for sexual habits. By employing these nine tests, the unqualified are discovered.

–Chuang Chou

His life was gentle, and the elements
So mix'd in him that Nature might stand up
And say to all the world, "This was a man!"

–Shakespeare

Sentimentality is a superstructure covering brutality.

—Carl G. Jung

It is easy—terribly easy—to shake a man's faith in himself. To take advantage of that to break a man's spirit is devil's work.

—George Bernard Shaw

Ethics according to Chung Yung, author of *The Unwobbling Pivot*: The archer, when he misses the bullseye, turns and seeks the cause of the error in himself.

—Ezra Pound

This glory and honor wherewith man is crowned ought to affect every person that is grateful, with celestial joy: and so much the rather because it is every man's proper and sole inheritance.

—Thomas Traherne

A man should never be ashamed to own he has been in the wrong, which is but saying in other words, that he is wiser today than he was yesterday.

—Jonathan Swift

Americans want to be loved; the English
want to be obeyed.

—Quentin Crisp

No man should advocate a course in private
that he's ashamed to admit in public.

—George McGovern

Nothing is more desirable than to be released
from an affliction, but nothing is more
frightening than to be divested of a crutch.

—James Baldwin

True contentment depends not upon what
we have; a tub was large enough for
Diogenes, but the world was too small for
Alexander.

—Charles Caleb Colton

There's nobody much that's impressed me as much as Shorty. Simple guy, but many is the poem I've written in my mind to the higher feelings he promoted in me—which he would have no ability whatsoever to articulate. If I sat down with Shorty in the spirit world or something and said, "Look, Shorty, here's what you really mean, as a prince of the world," he'd look at me like I was talking a foreign language.

. . . Now Shorty's not what a civics class would pick out as a role model. He was a featherbedded railroad brakeman, you know, who went to gin mills and drank and sat around all day with his shirt off and bullshitted. Everybody did love Shorty. . . . He wasn't a hidden man. It's not sentiment—this guy was advanced. Shorty just had a grasp—innate, not a conscious ability—about life.

—Jack Nicholson

Every difficulty slurred over will be a ghost to disturb your repose later on.

—Frederic Chopin

The psychic task which a person can and must set for himself is not to feel secure, but to be able to tolerate insecurity.

—Erich Fromm

How dare we bitch about our little problems when the people of Calcutta have lived with this misery for centuries and still find a way for radiance to come from their faces? . . . It blows the Western mind away.

—Patrick Swayze

Some trees grow very tall and straight and large in the forest close to each other, but some must stand by themselves or they won't grow at all.

—Oliver Wendell Holmes

We discover in ourselves what others hide from us, and we recognize in others what we hide from ourselves.

—Marquis de Vauvenargues

From without, no wonderful effect is
wrought within ourselves, unless some
interior, responding wonder meets it.

—Herman Melville

Excess on occasion is exhilarating. It
prevents moderation from acquiring the
deadening effect of a habit.

—W. Somerset Maugham

Kites rise against, not with the wind. No man
ever worked his passage anywhere in a dead
calm.

—John Neal

To know a truth well, one must have fought
it out.

—Novalis

If fate throws a knife at you, there are two ways of catching it—by the blade and by the handle.

—Oriental proverb

How should man, a being created in the likeness of God, live? What way of living is compatible with the grandeur and mystery of living?

—Abraham Joshua Heschel

WORK

A man who has no office to go to—I don't care who he is—is a trial of which you can have no conception.

–George Bernard Shaw

Every commodity is, as Marx says, a fetish, that is to say a non-existent penis. An investment. From feudal investiture to capitalistic investment, the manufacture of clothes for their own sake, not to be worn but to be saved in the hope chest. Instead of fixed robes and roles, fashion design and the endless search for identity: new personalities for old, turn in last year's model. The industrial revolution. Work is a masturbation dream, punishment for the Fall, which is falling asleep; and also a fall into division of the sexes.

–Norman O. Brown

There is no point in work
unless it absorbs you
like an absorbing game.

-D. H. Lawrence

It is more important to know the qualities and temperaments of people than those of stones and herbs. This is one of the subtlest things in life. Metals are identified by their sounds, and people by their speech. Words demonstrate integrity, and deeds even more so.

-Baltasar Gracián

I made up a new proverb: "Indians chase the vision, white men chase the dollar." We are lousy raw material from which to form a capitalist. We could do it easily, but then we would stop being Indians. We would just be ordinary citizens with a slightly darker skin. That's a high price to pay, my friend, too high. We make lousy farmers too, because deep down within us lingers a feeling that land, water, air, the earth and what lies beneath its surface cannot be owned as someone's private property. That belongs to everybody, and if man wants to survive, he had better come around to this Indian point of view, the sooner the better, because there isn't much time left to think it over.

-John (Fire) Lame Deer

A man is happy when, far from the business
    world,
  like the earliest tribe of men
he cultivates the family farm with his team,
  and is free from usury's ties—

—Horace

Money, to be worth striving for, must have
blood and perspiration on it—preferably that
of someone else.

—Wilson Mizner

If a politician found he had cannibals among
his constituents, he would promise them
missionaries for dinner.

—H. L. Mencken

All things considered, work is less boring
than amusing oneself.

—Charles Baudelaire

Hard work is damn near as overrated as
monogamy.

—Huey P. Long

I have a horror of all the professions. Masters
and workers, all just base peasants. The hand
with a pen equals the hand with a plow.
What a century of hands! I'll never learn to
use my hands. But then, domesticity goes too
far. The straightforwardness of beggary turns
my stomach. Criminals are as disgusting as
castrates: as for me, I am intact, and I don't
care.

—Arthur Rimbaud

Nature serves to notify us, by way of savages
and children, that our industrial method is
contrary to her design. When children want
to work on Sundays, and savages want to
labor and plant, we will be able to believe
that humanity has taken nature's path, that it
has at last discovered its destiny.

—Charles Fourier

If you are going to sin, sin against God, not
the bureaucracy. God will forgive you but
the bureaucracy won't.

—Hyman Rickover

So, as Lazarus walks thru villages, so God
walks thru our lives, and like the workers
and the warriors we worry like worrywarts
to straighten up the damage as fast as we
can, tho the whole thing's hopeless in the
end. For God has a bigger foot than Lazarus
and all the Texcocos and Texacos and
Mañanas of tomorrow.

—Jack Kerouac

Meetings are an addictive, highly
self-indulgent activity that corporations and
other large organizations habitually engage in
only because they cannot actually
masturbate.

—Dave Barry

No bird soars too high, if he soars with his
    own wings.

The most sublime act is to set another before
    you.

If the fool would persist in his folly he would
    become wise.

—William Blake

My young men shall never work. Men who
work cannot dream, and wisdom comes in
dreams.

You ask me to plow the ground. Shall
I take a knife and tear my mother's breast?
Then when I die she will not take me to her
bosom to rest.

You ask me to dig for stone. Shall I
dig under her skin for bones? Then when I
die I cannot enter her body to be born again.

You ask me to cut grass and make
hay and sell it, and be rich like white men.
But how dare I cut off my mother's hair?

It is a bad law, and my people cannot
obey it. I want my people to stay with me
here. All the dead men will come to life
again. We must wait here in the house of our
fathers and be ready to meet them in the
body of our mother.

—Smohalla

What the Mole Said
I hate the sun,
all that commotion.

I want to grind steadily
at the roots of darkness.

Work is my salvation.

—Michael Hannon

From *The Wisdom of the Tao*
Cook Ting was cutting up an ox for Lord
Wen-hui. Wherever his hand touched the ox,
or his shoulder leaned against it, or his foot
held it down, or his knee kneeled against it,
he slithered the knife along with a zing, and
all was in perfect rhythm, as though he were
performing the dance of the *Mulberry Grove*
or keeping time to the *Ching-shou* music.

"Ah, this is marvelous!" said Lord
Wen-hui. "How did you ever achieve such
skill?"

Cook Ting laid down his knife and
replied, "What I care about is the Way of
Tao, which goes beyond skill. When I first
began cutting up oxen, all I could see was the
whole oxen. After three years I no longer
saw the whole oxen. Now I proceed by

intuition and don't look with my eyes, for when a sense organ ceases to function, Spirit takes over. Relying upon the natural form of the oxen's body, I strike the big hollows and pass through the large crevices. Following along in this way, the veins, arteries, and tendons are never touched at all, and the big bones go untouched competely!"

"A good cook changes his knife once a year—because he hacks. A mediocre cook will change his knife every month, because he has been breaking bones with it. But I've had this knife of mine for nineteen years and I've cut up thousands of oxen with it, and the blade is as good as the day it left the grindstone. Know that there exist spaces between the joints, and that the blade of a knife has no thickness. If you insert what has no thickness into those spaces, there's plenty of room—more than enough for the blade to move in! That's why after nineteen years the edge of my blade is still as good as the day it left the grindstone.

"However, whenever I come to a complicated place, I size up the difficulties, and proceed with caution. I fix my gaze and go slowly. Then, I barely move my blade, and whump! The difficulty comes apart like a clod of earth crumbling to the ground.

Afterwards I stand with my knife in my
hand, and look all around me elatedly. Then
I wipe the knife clean and put it away."

"That's it!" exclaimed Lord Wen-hui.
"Your words have shown me how I ought to
live my life!"

—Chuang Chou

Work for this world as if you will live
forever—and work for the next world as if
you will die tomorrow.

—The Prophet Muhammad

Work as if you were to live 100 years, Pray
as if you were to die Tomorrow.

—Benjamin Franklin

The best way out is always through.

—Robert Frost

We have all grown up with the mythology of hunting. In fantasy, we may be cavemen with spears, or Indians with bows and arrows—in reality, we take our rod and reel down to a wharf or local fishing hole and throw in a line. The very nature of hunting and fishing calls up deep echoes within us—are ancestral hunters stalking through our male DNA memories, silently following a deer, or scooping salmon from a stream with bare hands?

The act of hunting has shifted from necessity to sport. Modern society has domesticated our food sources and created the idea of hunting as leisure. Men can now go off on woodland hunts and come back with edible trophies. Some among us have developed a keen sense of hunter's morality—similar to that of the Native Americans who hunted this country's wildlife before us. These men hunted only what they could use, and sought a creaturely kinship with the targeted animal before taking its life.

But for most of us who live the modern urban life, our main manly hunt circles around job, identity, or the perfect mate. But there is still a powerful mystique attached to hunting. It is a unique time when a man, alone, comes face to face with a life whose fate lies in his hands. He is at the mercy of the moment, dependent on his own skill and keenness—his senses alert, his intellect sharp.

Whatever we hunt and however we see the hunt, it takes all our skill and patience. Just as we may capture a deer in the cross hairs of our sights, so are we also in the middle of those cross hairs, expected to prove ourselves successful hunters. The empty-handed hunter is a pathetic figure; a man can't return empty-handed too often without undergoing a psychic revolution in his image of himself. After all, the woods are dark and full of game, and the sea is full of fish. Our eyes are aglitter with the challenge to come back with what we have caught by our own resourceful cunning.

For me, trout fishing is the only place I get
what you're supposed to get in church.

—Tom McGuane

Men that are taken to be grave, because
nature hath made them of a sour complexion;
money-getting men, men that spend all their
time, first in getting, and next in anxious care
to keep it; men that are condemned to be
rich, and then always busy or discontented;
for these poor rich men, we Anglers pity
them perfectly, and stand in no need to
borrow their thought to think ourselves so
happy. No, no, sir, we enjoy a contentedness
above the reach of such dispositions.

—Isaak Walton

The gods do not deduct from man's allotted
span the hours spent in fishing.

—Babylonian proverb

If God didn't want man to hunt, he wouldn't
have given us plaid shirts.

—Johnny Carson

The greatest hunter in the village where I lived was an old man named Wesley Ekak. His sense of animals was so profound that the distinction between his humanness and the animal's animalness seemed blurred. One spring, for example, we were camped on the edge of the ice, hunting for whales. We hadn't seen one in three or four days because the ice south of us had closed up. There were six or seven of us inside the tent, and the old man—he must have been about seventy at the time—was lying on his caribou-skin mattress with his eyes closed, smoking a cigarette. Suddenly he said, "I think a whale is going to come." Then, after a short time, "I think it's going to come up really close." To my amazement, all the men raced to ready their hunting gear. I felt so ridiculous that I got up too. I remember saying to Ekak, who was the only person who hadn't moved at all, "Well, I guess I'll go out and see if you're right." Before I got five steps out of the tent, a whale blew right in front of me, just off the ice.

It was the only whale we saw in three days. No one mentioned a word about it except Ekak, who said later, "There was a ringing in my ears."

—Jonathan White

With a Telescope Rod on Cowiche Creek
Here my assurance drops away. I lose
all direction. Gray Lady
onto moving waters. My thoughts
stir like ruffed grouse
in the clearing across the creek.

Suddenly, as at a signal, the birds
pass silently back into pine trees.

—Raymond Carver

There is, or should be, a rhythmic evolution
to the fisherman's life (there is so little
rhythm today in so many lives). At first
glance it may seem merely that from barefoot
boy with garden hackle to fly-fisherman with
all the delicious paraphernalia that makes
trout fishing a consummate ritual, an enticing
and inexhaustible mystery, a perpetual
delight. But the evolution runs deeper, and
incorporates at least at one level an
increasing respect for the "event" of fishing (I
would not even call it "sport") and of nature,
and a diminishing of much necessary interest
in the fat creel.

—Nick Lyons

"Aye, breach your last to the sun, Moby Dick!" cried Ahab, "thy hour and thy harpoon are at hand!—Down! down all of ye, but one man at the fore. The boats!—stand by!"

—Herman Melville

Black-tailed Deer Song
Down from the houses of magic,
    Down from the houses of magic
Blow the winds, and from my antlers
    And my ears they stronger gather.

Over there I ran trembling,
    Over there I ran trembling,
For bows and arrows pursued me.
    Many bows were on my trail.

—Pima Indian song

From *The Island Within*
Inching like a reptile on a cold rock, I have stepped out from the tree and let my whole menacing profile become visible. The deer are thirty feet away and stand well apart, so they can both see me easily. I am a hunter hovering near his prey and a watcher craving inhuman love, torn between the deepest

impulses, hot and shallow-breathed and seething with unreconciled intent, hidden from opened eyes that look into the nimbus of sun and see nothing but the shadow they have chosen for themselves. In this shadow now, the hunter has vanished and only the watcher remains.

Drawn by the honey of the doe's scent, the buck steps quickly toward her. And now the most extraordinary thing happens. The doe turns away from him and walks straight for me. There is no hesitation, only a wild deer coming along the trail of hardened snow where the other deer have passed, the trail in which I stand at this moment. She raises her head, looks at me, and steps without pausing.

My existence is reduced to a pair of eyes; a rush of unbearable heat flushes through my cheeks; and a sense of absolute certainty fuses in my mind.

The snow blazes so brightly that my head aches. The deer is a dark form growing larger. I look up at the buck, half embarrassed, as if to apologize that she's chosen me over him. He stares at her for a moment, turns to follow, then stops and watches anxiously. I am struck by how gently her hoofs touch the trail, how little sound they make as she steps, how thick the fur is on her flank and shoulder, how unfathomable her eyes look. I am consumed with a sense of her perfect elegance in the brilliant light. And then I am lost again in the whirling intensity of experience.

The doe is now ten feet from me. She never pauses or looks away. Her feet punch down mechanically into the snow, coming closer and closer, until they are less than a yard from my own. Then she stops, stretches her neck calmly toward me, and lifts her nose.

There is not the slightest question in my mind, as if this was sure to happen and I have known all along exactly what to do. I slowly raise my hand and reach out.

And my fingers touch the soft, dry, gently needling fur on top of the deer's head, and press down to the living warmth of flesh underneath.

She makes no move and shows no fear, but I can feel the flaming strength and tension that flow in her wild body as in no other animal I have touched. Time expands and I am suspended in the clear reality of the moment.

Then, by the flawed conditioning of a lifetime among fearless domesticated things, I instinctively drop my hand and let the deer smell it. Her black nose, wet and shining, touches gently against my skin at the exact instant I realize the absoluteness of my error. And a tremor runs through her entire body as she realizes hers. Her muscles seize and harden; she seems to wrench her eyes away from me but her body remains, rigid and paralyzed. Having been deceived by her other senses, she keeps her nose tight against my hand for one more moment.

Then all the energy inside her triggers in a series of exquisite bounds. She flings out over the hummocks of snow-covered moss, suspended in effortless flight like fog blown over the muskeg in a gale. Her body leaps with such power that the muscles should twang aloud, like a bowstring; the earth should shudder and drum; but I hear no sound. In the center of the muskeg she stops to look back, as if to confirm what must seem impossible. The buck follows in more earthbound undulations; they dance away together, and I am left in the meeting place alone.

—Richard Nelson

Those who would hunt a man need to remember that a jungle also contains those who hunt the hunters.

—Malcolm X

And where is the hunter who is cunning?
    The practical part of me?
Oh he is long since gone, dispersed among
    the bold grasses.
The one he does not know of remains afloat
    and awake all night;
he lies on luminous boulders, dives, his coat
    sleek, his eyes open.

                              –Robert Bly

In matters of love, we might be even more romantic than women. The history of the world is studded with tales of man's toil, struggle, and eventual self-sacrifice for love—for a woman, for one's country, for an ideal. We thirst for and express deep love with a daredevil's intensity and an aerialist's agility. Even when our impulses are a bit boyish, even when we take the whole matter too seriously, we have a consuming need for love to flow toward us, and to let our own love flow.

Some men, in great equilibrium and balance, exude a physical glow of compassion and worldly love. Like Zorba the Greek, they love life, wine, their work, old women, dance—everybody and everything. They are like saints of the sensual. Their bodies seem to swim in love's atmosphere, and anyone who comes near them is affected by its pungent releases. These are men completely in touch with their hearts.

Others feel love in surges. We fall in love and enter a glowing, glorious cosmos, and fall out of love onto the hard asphalt of dreary every day. Sometimes we are drawn to love by the head, sometimes by the heart, sometimes by the sly Don Juan between our thighs.

And then there is the not-too-distant cousin of Eros, **Neurosis**. Some of us flee from love's touch for a maze of reasons, or shy away from a commitment that looms over us like car payments. Some of us do everything we can to unconsciously ward off love, while we consciously long for it with all our hearts. In the end, we must have enough faith in ourselves (and in whatever God of Love we believe in) to dare to love.

To see a man in a state of realized, pure love is to see someone who's simplified everything. If he has a family, his great arms and shoulders surround it with a warm protection, and his children go out into the world transmitting their father's loving confidence. Such a man becomes the giant redwood tree watching at the edge of a glade—a lover like nature itself, nourisher and guard.

I have met on the street a very poor man
who was in love. His hat was old, his coat
was out at the elbows, the water passed
through his shoes, and the stars through his
soul.

—Victor Hugo

I love you with a love that never fades
    though some men's loves are mere
    midday mirages.
A portrait of you rides here in my heart
    with my pure love for you inscribed
    beneath it.
Nothing in my soul but you, but if
    there were I'd pluck it out at once,
    with my bare hands!
I ask you only for your love, that's all.
   And if I should possess it, then—
All the world would be a senile camel to me,
   All mankind like floating motes
   of dust,
All the world's people buzzing 'round
   like insects.

—Ibn Hazm

I'll tell ya—yeah, I'm in love. Those are the
things that, when you're at the other end of
the scale, you know, and you think, "Oh,
god*damn*, you can only be in love when
you're eighteen or twenty-three. . . . But then
you get older and suddenly—*bang*! One
again! And you realize that was all a load of
crap. And those are the things that turn you
on, you know? Those are the things that
make you look forward, keep you going. You
say, well if it *can* happen, keep on going. I
mean, it's the greatest feeling in the world,
right? . . . Love wears a white Stetson.

—Keith Richards

I no longer love her, that's certain, but
　　　maybe I love her.
Love is so short, and forgetting so long.

—Pablo Neruda

A body is a body. A woman could be deaf,
dumb, crippled, and blind and still have soul
and compassion. That's all that matters to
me. You can hear it in the voice.

—Bob Dylan

A beautiful woman who is pleasing to men is
good only for frightening fish when she falls
into the water.

—Zen proverb

All girls should have a poem
written for them even if
we have to turn this God-damn world
upside down to do it.

—Richard Brautigan

The repose of love is a weariness; its onset, a
        sickness; its end, death.
For me, however, death through love is life;
        I give thanks to my Beloved that she
                has held it out to me.
Whoever does not die of his love is unable to
        live by it.

—Ibn al-Farid

We all have eyes for our own Dark Angel.

—Arthur Rimbaud

Song

Mother sister beautiful companion of the
    night

again and again you wound me kiss me heal
    me

and try to say that because nothing is held
nothing can be lost.

Often I feel that I am only
the clarity of my pain held aloft
like a verse not to be spoken.

Mother sister beautiful companion of the
    night

keep playing please that deliberate music
which binds me to the dream of your free
    body.

                                          —Michael Hannon

Love is all fire; and so heaven and hell are the
same place. As in Augustine, the torments of
the damned are part of the felicity of the
redeemed. Two cities; which are one city.
Eden is a fiery city; just like hell.

                                          —Norman O. Brown

Whenever a man encounters a woman in a
mood he doesn't understand, he wants to
know if she is tired.

—George Jean Nathan

Among those I like, I can find no common
denominator, but among those I love I can:
all of them made me laugh.

—W. H. Auden

I've seen the whole world. I learn somethin'
from people everywhere. There's truth in
Hinduism, Christianity, Islam, all religions.
And in just plain talkin'. What I've found is
that the religion that matters, the real
religion, is love.

—Muhammad Ali

These people [the Indians of Hispaniola] love
their neighbors as themselves; their discourse
is ever sweet and gentle, and accompanied
by a smile. I swear to your majesties, there is
not in the world a better nation or a better
land.

—Christopher Columbus

Affection is the basis for the creation of the entire universe, all beings and creatures. Everything has affection as its base and foundation. Affection is the marrow and essence of all worlds, visible or invisible, known or unknown. Affection is the secret of creation.

—Sheikh Muzaffer Ozak al-Jerrahi

Unless the mind be trained to selflessness and infinite compassion, one is apt to fall into the error of seeking liberation for self alone.

—Gampopa

The law of love will work, just as the law of gravitation will work, whether we accept it or not. . . . the force of non-violence is infinitely more wonderful and subtle than the material forces of nature, like, for instance, electricity. The men who discovered for us the law of love were greater scientists than any of our modern scientists.

—Mahatma Gandhi

We may even want to be good soldiers and skillful, invincible warriors. Or we may not want to study war at all—perhaps we're so traumatized by the wars of the twentieth century that we want to use only peaceful means to settle differences. "Police actions" like Vietnam and the threat of total human annihilation have cooled many of us to the idea of any kind of war—at any time, in any place.

Still, warring ways haunt us—from the mean streets of our cities to other males' macho proddings. We are taught early that "real men" are strong, aggressive, and defend what belongs to them. The wild ones among us extend this lesson, and take everything they **think** belongs to them, whether or not it actually does. In short: we remain warlike.

Some of us feel inadequate if we do not live up to a warrior-like image. But there are many ways to go to war. There's the fight for justice, or for the rights of the oppressed, or for feeding the hungry. Some of us go into business with a warlike strategy in mind, and prove our valor in boardrooms. Victory comes by valiantly clinching deals.

Then there is another war, often said to be the most difficult one to wage. This is the inner war: the battle against all of the bad qualities in **ourselves**. But this war takes place on a spiritual battlefield. It may be harder to fight our demons than to confront any material adversary.

Whichever war we wage, we might remember what Alexander the Great's teacher, Aristotle (384–322 B.C.), said: "War must be for the sake of peace, business for the sake of leisure, and all things necessary and useful for the sake of things noble."

Never give a sword to a man who can't
dance.

—Celtic motto

Once there was a man who owned a fine
hunting horse. It was black and fast and
afraid of nothing. When it was turned upon
an enemy it charged in a straight line and
struck at full speed; the man need have no
hand upon the rein. But, you know, that man
knew fear. Once during a charge he turned
that animal from its course. That was a bad
thing. The hunting horse died of shame.

—N. Scott Momaday

I do not favor battles, particularly at the
beginning of a war. I am sure a good general
can make war *all his life* and not be
compelled to fight one.

—Marshal de Saxe

You can always tell an old soldier by the
inside of his holsters and cartridge boxes.
The young ones carry pistols and cartridges:
the old ones, grub.

— George Bernard Shaw

They went without shields, and were mad as
dogs or wolves, and bit on their shields, and
were as strong as bears or bulls; men they
slew, and neither fire nor steel would deal
with them; and this is what is called the fury
of the beserker.

—The Völsunga Saga, Scandanavian prose cycle

The self-confidence of the warrior is not the
self-confidence of the average man. The
average man seeks certainty in the eyes of
the onlooker and calls that self-confidence.
The warrior seeks impeccability in his own
eyes and calls that humbleness. The average
man is hooked to his fellow men, while the
warrior is hooked to himself.

—Carlos Castaneda

. . . It is
Good to be brave—nothing is
Better. Food tastes better. Wine
Is more brilliant. Girls are more
Beautiful. The sky is bluer . . .

—Kenneth Rexroth

The military is the modern way to carry on
warrior traditions. They can't go on horse
raids anymore.

— Ben Nighthorse Campbell

They'd talk about physical wounds in one
way and psychic wounds in another, each
man in a squad would tell you how crazy
everyone else in the squad was, everyone
knew grunts who'd gone crazy in the middle
of a firefight, gone crazy on patrol, gone
crazy back at camp, gone crazy on R&R, gone
crazy during their first month home. Going
crazy was built into the tour, the best you
could hope for was that it didn't happen
around you, the kind of crazy that made men
empty clips into strangers or fix grenades on
latrine doors. That was *really* crazy; anything
less was almost standard, as standard as the
vague prolonged stares and involuntary
smiles, common as ponchos or 16s or any
other piece of war issue.

— Michael Herr

As long as war is looked upon as wicked, it will always have its fascination. When it is looked upon as vulgar, it will cease to be popular.

—Oscar Wilde

From *The Marvels of War*

To the future I leave the history of
    Guillaume Apollinaire
Who was in the war and knew how to be
    everywhere
In happy villages behind the lines
In all the rest of the universe
In those who died tangled in barbed wire
In the women the cannon and the horses
At the zenith and the nadir and at the four
    cardinal points
And in the singular heat on the eve of this
    battle
And it would undoubtedly be even more
    beautiful
If I could suppose that all these things in
    which I am everywhere
Could also be in me
But nothing is made this way
For if I am everywhere right this minute
    there is still only I who is in me

—Guillaume Apollinaire

Be your Self, at war with oneself.

—Coomaraswamy

Knowledge, riches, high office, rank and
    good fortune are just mischief in the
    hands of evil-natured men.
So true believers must do battle from time to
    time to snatch away sharp spears from
    the hands of madmen.

—Jalaluddin Rumi

Perhaps people think that I have come to
bring peace to the world. They do not know
that I have come to bring conflict to the
earth: fire, sword, war. For five people will
be in a house: it will be three against two,
and two against three, father against son and
son against father, and they will stand alone.

—The Secret Sayings of Jesus

. . . if angels fight,
Weak men must fall, for heaven still guards
  the right.

–William Shakespeare

There is no greater victory in the life of a
human being than victory over the mind. He
who has controlled the gusts of passion that
arise within him and the violent actions that
proceed therefrom is the real hero.

–Swami Ramdas

A warrior did much more than fight. . . .
Warriors fed their families and washed the
dishes. Warriors went on Vision Quests and
listened to their wives when they went on
Vision Quests, too. Warriors picked up their
dirty clothes and tried not to watch football
games all weekend.

–Sherman Alexie

Tell a man he is brave, and you help him to
become so.

–Thomas Carlyle

If we could read the secret history of our enemies, we should find in each man's life sorrow and suffering enough to disarm all hostility.

—Henry Wadsworth Longfellow

When you have no choice, mobilize the spirit of courage.

—Jewish proverb

. . . my grandpa Good Fox played a big part in my life, and I looked up to him. He had a great reputation as a warrior, but he was not a killing man. Most of his war honors came from "counting coup," riding up to the enemy, zig-zagging among them, touching them with his crooked cup stick wrapped in otter fur. He was a coup-man. That was his way of showing his bravery.

—John (Fire) Lame Deer

You fall out of your mother's womb, you crawl across open country under fire, and drop into your grave.

—Quentin Crisp

In Confucianism, all of us—men and women—are born soldiers. The soldier is the universal individual. No matter what you do for a living—doctor, lawyer, fisherman, thief—you are a fighter. Life is war. The war is to maintain personal integrity in a world that demands betrayal and corruption. All behavior is strategy and tactics. All relationships are martial. Marriages are military alliances.

—Frank Chin

I have given two cousins to war and I stand ready to sacrifice my wife's brother.

—Artemus Ward

To die for an idea; it is unquestionably noble. But how much nobler it would be if men died for ideas that were true!

—H. L. Mencken

If they really want to honor the soldiers, why don't they let them sit in the stands and have the people march by?

—Will Rogers

The problem is not the war but the
perversion. And the perversion is a
repression; war is sex perverted.

> —Norman O. Brown

War is energy Enslav'd.

> —William Blake

Self-conquest is the greatest of all victories.

> —Plato

War Song

Let us see, is this real,
Let us see, is this real,
This life I am living?
Ye Gods, who dwell everywhere,
Let us see, is this real,
This life I am living?

> —Pawnee war song

A great part of our lives as men entails a quest. We go after what appears inaccessible and achieve it—or at least deepen ourselves in the attempt. Often the quest is not for material comforts or worldly success, but for something much greater, something harder to define. The visionary quest may be a search for one's deepest reality. It may be an intellectual search or an artistic search. Or it may be a struggle to align ourselves, beyond even our masculine identities, with the great Void—the Light of the heavens and earth—to let go of our separate identities altogether.

Some cultures feature this quest openly in their social traditions. But most western cultures look upon the visionary quest as sheer madness or as dangerous to the "rest of us." Such attitudes discourage the men who yearn to set out in a new, truer direction. So many men must take this quest privately, at the very fringes of society. Translating the results into socially acceptable language can be a source of anguish and frustration for the journeyman.

At a less radical extreme, all men seek something that men sought before them—something that beckons them on. Perhaps it's their role in the future, or perhaps it's a childhood dream. Perhaps it's a complex search for the answers to the mysteries of the universe, or perhaps it's a simpler quest—a quest to beautifully and successfully maintain a family. A sane and fulfilling life can be the most challenging quest of all.

The spiritual quest may bring us to a point of gratitude, worship, and enlightenment—it may bring us to a nakedness of soul and openness of heart. The road that winds from the boy with a dirty face and puckish grin to the illumined man at ease in the world can be a long one— but it is traversable within each of our lifetimes.

And that may be the quest we're here for after all.

Begin where you are.

—Sam Keen

When man sings birds humble into piety;
What history can the whale empire sing?
What genius ant dare break from anthood
As can man from manhood?

—Gregory Corso

Man is the dwarf of himself. Once he was
permeated and dissolved by spirit. He filled
nature with his overflowing currents. Out
from him sprang the sun and moon. . . . The
laws of his mind, the periods of his actions
externalized themselves into day and night,
into the year and the seasons. But, having
made for himself this huge shell, his waters
retired; he no longer fills the veins and
veinlets; he is shrunk to a drop. He sees, that
the structure still fits him, but fits him
colossally. Say, rather, once it fitted him,
now it corresponds to him from far and on
high.

—Ralph Waldo Emerson

Any life, no matter how long and complex it may be, is made up of a *single moment*—the moment in which a man finds out, once and for all, who he is.

—Jorge Luis Borges

Each moment is the fruit of forty thousand years.

—Thomas Wolfe

If we are always arriving and departing, it is also true that we are eternally anchored. One's destination is never a place but rather a new way of looking at things.

—Henry Miller

It's in the darkness of men's eyes that they get lost.

—Black Elk

We must be fond of the world, even in order to change it.

—G. K. Chesterton

I can only say that I am no prophet, I am but an erring mortal, progressing from blunder towards truth.

—Mahatma Gandhi

Greatness is a transitory experience.

—Frank Herbert

The grail, the grail! It fills one's mind in the early morning as one's skin is filled with ardor. There is no question of compromise or defeat. One wants only to make an exemplary contribution, and if this is accomplished one's ending is inconsequential!

—John Cheever

. . . who drove cross-country seventy-two
  hours to find out if I had a vision or you
  had a vision or he had a vision to find
  out Eternity...

—Allen Ginsberg

This image made to the image of God in the first shaping was wonderly fair and bright, full of burning love and ghostly light.

—Walter Hilton

The man without imagination has no wings,
he cannot fly.

–Muhammad Ali

The Imagination makes us transcendant of
Time and we see what is gorgeous.

–Michael McClure

We are what we imagine. Our very existence
consists in our imagination of ourselves. . . .
The greatest tragedy that can befall us is to
go unimagined.

–N. Scott Momaday

The basis of action is lack of imagination. It
is the last resource of those who know not
how to dream.

–Oscar Wilde

There are no mistakes and it's never boring
on the edge of the imagination, which is only
pure spirit out having a bit of fun.

–Hugh Romney [Wavy Gravy]

How many lazy men's truths have been admitted in the name of imagination! How often has the term imagination been used to prettify the unhealthy tendency of the soul to soar off in a boundless quest after truth, leaving the body where it always was!

—Yukio Mishima

A man gazing at the stars is proverbially at the mercy of the puddles in the road.

—Alexander Smith

"You must learn to look at the world twice," Indian elders advise. First you must bring your eyes together in front so you can see each droplet of rain on the grass, so you can see the smoke rising from an ant hill in the sunshine. *Nothing* should escape your notice. But you must learn to look again, with your eyes at the very edge of what is visible. Now you must see dimly if you wish to see things that are dim—visions, mist, and cloud people, animals which hurry past you in the dark. You must learn to look at the world twice if you wish to see all that there is to see.

—Jamake Highwater

Let him who seeks not cease seeking until he
    finds.
And when he finds, he will be dismayed.
And if he is dismayed, he will be amazed,
and he will be king over All.

—The Secret Sayings of Jesus

THE ARTISTIC LIFE

My first acting teacher said all art is one thing—a stimulating point of departure. That's it. And if you can do that in a piece, you've fulfilled your cultural, sociological obligation as a workman. What you're supposed to do is keep people vitally interested in the world they live in. Artists are supposed to be of use, to make people not necessarily happy, but enrich their vitality.

—Jack Nicholson

All these youngsters think they can build on emptiness. Nothing emerges from nothing. You must be humble and not think that you know. Everything must be begun again . . . and I who have waited until seventy to go to Italy!

—Georges Rouault

We cannot express the light in nature
because we have not the sun. We can only
express the light we have in ourselves.

–Arthur Dove

Earthly life is an eternal miracle. In a
moment of grace, we can grasp eternity in
the palm of our hand. This is the gift given to
creative individuals who can identify with
the mysteries of life through art. It is a divine
gift, this spirit of humanity. It is the fight for
light over shadow.

–Marcel Marceau

Hell, we artists are not normal people. You
can't do the same type of stuff with artists
that you do with other people.

–Miles Davis

I like the lifestyle in Italy. I like a siesta. I like the way that living your life becomes an art in itself. In America you can lose track of that; everything's based on the values of success.

—Matt Dillon

The most sublime labor of poetry is to give sense and passion to insensate things; and it is characteristic of children to take inanimate things in their hands and talk to them in play as if they were living persons . . . in the world's childhood, men were by nature sublime poets. . . .

—Giambattista Vico

Really great works have a serene look. Through small openings one perceives precipices; down at the bottom there is darkness, vertigo; but above the whole soars something singularly sweet. That is the ideal of light, the smiling of the sun; and how calm it is, calm and strong!

—Gustave Flaubert

Has anyone at the end of the nineteenth century a distinct conception of what poets of strong ages called *inspiration*? If not, I will describe it. If one had the slightest residue of superstition left in one, one would hardly be able to set aside the idea that one is merely incarnation, merely mouthpiece, merely medium of overwhelming forces. The concept of revelation, in the sense that something suddenly, with unspeakable certainty and subtlety, becomes *visible*, audible, something that shakes and overturns one to the depths, simply describes the fact. One hears, one does not seek; one takes, one does not ask who gives; a thought flashes up like lightning, with necessity, unfalteringly formed—I have never had any choice. . . . Everything is in the highest degree involuntary but takes place as in a tempest of a feeling of freedom, of absoluteness, of power, of divinity. . . . The involuntary nature of image, of metaphor is the most remarkable thing of all; one no longer has any idea what is image, what metaphor, everything presents itself as the readiest, the truest, the simplest means of expression.

—Friedrich Nietzsche

The Artist at Fifty

The crow nests high in the fir.
Birds leap through the snowy branches
uttering small cries. Clumps fall.
Mice run dragging their tails in the
    new-fallen snow.

Year after year the artist works,
early and late, studying the old.
What does he gain? Finally he dreams
one night of deer antlers abandoned in the
    snow.

—Robert Bly

THE INTELLECTUAL LIFE

The only journey of knowledge is from the depth of one being to the heart of another.

—Norman Mailer

Sometimes it proves the highest understanding not to understand.

—Baltasar Gracián

On earth, man wears himself out in intellectual adventures, as though seeking to take wing and fly to infinity. Motionless before his desk, he edges his way closer, ever closer, to the borders of the spirit, in constant mortal danger of plunging into the void. At such times—though very rarely—the spirit, too, has its glimpses of the dawn light.

—Yukio Mishima

The test of a first-rate intelligence is the ability to hold two opposed ideas in the mind at the same time, and still retain the ability to function.

—F. Scott Fitzgerald

Philosophy cannot be the same after Auschwitz and Hiroshima. Certain assumptions about humanity have proved to be specious, have been smashed. What has long been regarded as commonplace has proved to be utopianism.

—Abraham Joshua Heschel

You can't oppose something intellectually that is overwhelming you emotionally. The chain of command, or the chain of action, comes up from the viscera to the back brain and then finally to the front brain. But the front brain cannot reverse this and give orders to the back brain and the viscera; it just doesn't work. "Pull yourself together!" they say. Well, you can't. The more you try to pull yourself together the further apart you get. You have to learn to let the thing pass through.

—William S. Burroughs

The important thing is not to stop
questioning.

> —Albert Einstein

I do not know what I may appear to the
world, but to myself I seem to have been
only a child playing on the seashore while
the great ocean of truth lay all undiscovered
before me.

> —Sir Isaac Newton

If we do discover a complete theory, it
should in time be understandable in broad
principle by everyone, not just a few
scientists. Then we shall all, philosophers,
scientists, and just ordinary people, be able
to take part in the discussion of the question
of why it is that we and the universe exist. If
we find the answer to that, it would be the
ultimate triumph of human reason—for then
we would know the mind of God.

> —Stephen W. Hawking

An elephant in a dark barn: some Hindus
    were putting it on display.

In order to see it, people had to go into
    the dark.

Unable to see it with their eyes, they had to
    feel it with the palms of their hands.

One person's hand felt along the trunk: "This
    beast's shaped like a waterpipe!"

Someone else felt its ear: "It's shaped like
    a fan!"

Another felt its leg: "An elephant's built like
    a pillar!"

Yet another felt along its back, and said: "Ha!
    An elephant is just like a giant chair!"

So anyone who heard what an elephant was
    understood it purely from the part that
    person touched.

Depending on their point of view, their ideas
    differed—one person saw it as hunched,
    another as straight.

If only each had held a candle in his hand,
    their dispute would have been over!

—Jalaluddin Rumi

It is better to understand little than to
misunderstand a lot.

—Anatole France

155

It is well enough known, that the best productions of the best human intellects are generally regarded by those intellects as mere immature freshman exercises, wholly worthless in themselves, except as initiatives for entering the great University of God after death.

—Herman Melville

The best thing for being sad is to learn something. That is the only thing that never fails.

—T. H. White

I would just like to *study*. I mean ranging study, because I have a wideopen mind. I'm interested in almost any subject you can mention. I know this is the reason I have come to really like, as individuals, some of the hosts of radio or television panel programs I have been on, and to respect their minds—because even if they have been almost steadily in disagreement with me on the race issue, they still have kept their minds open and objective about the truths of things happening in this world.

—Malcolm X

If you leave the smallest corner of your head
vacant for a moment, other people's opinions
will rush in from all quarters.

–George Bernard Shaw

You can control the mind only by keeping it
occupied with the mirror of wisdom. There is
no other way. It is impossible to overcome it
because it contains so many millions of
monkeys and tricks.

–Bawa Muhaiyaddeen

I can't understand why people are frightened
of new ideas. I'm frightened of the old ones.

–John Cage

Cynicism—the intellectual cripple's
substitute for intelligence.

–Russell Lynes

He who Doubts from what he sees
Will ne'er Believe, do what you Please.
If the Sun & Moon should doubt,
They'd immediately Go out.

–William Blake

Tim was so learned, that he could name a
Horse in nine Languages. So ignorant, that he
bought a Cow to ride on.

—Benjamin Franklin

You cannot teach a man anything; you can
only help him find it within himself.

—Galileo

All are lunatics, but he who can analyze his
delusions is called a philosopher.

—Ambrose Bierce

Too bad that all the people who know how to
run the country are busy driving taxicabs and
cutting hair.

—George Burns

SPIRITUALITY

Could a greater miracle take place than for us
to look through each other's eyes for an
instant?

—Henry David Thoreau

I had more powerful spiritual experiences
back a few years ago, when I had my first
encounters with the mountains and the
oceans. It was just a matter of being high and
seeing a different order—as opposed to
whatever the hell I knew when I was
eighteen years old. School and lunch. And
beer. Aside from those three, I didn't have
much experience. And girls. So there was
just something different happening. I saw
there was something else to see. I can't
describe it. It's just a better feeling than
usual. And yet it's perfectly ordinary
because it's intended to be perfectly
ordinary. It's not like lightning bolts hitting
you on the head. It's not flying. It's just
different.

—Bill Murray

Once I forgave dogs, and pitied men, sat
in the rain counting Juju beads, raindrops
are ecstasy, ecstasy is raindrops. . . .

—Jack Kerouac

Happy the man who is busy attending to
what God is saying in him. He is directly
subject to the divine light-ray. The soul that
stands with all her powers under the light of
God is fired and inflamed with divine love.
The divine light shines straight in from
above, and a perpendicular sun on one's
head is a thing that few can survive. Yet the
highest power of the soul, her head, is held
erect beneath this shaft of godly light so that
there can shine in this light divine which I
have oft described as being so bright, so
overwhelming, so transcendant, that all lights
are but darkness in comparison with this
light.

—Meister Eckhart

When it is dark enough you can see the stars.

—Ralph Waldo Emerson

There are *two* struggles—inner-world struggle
and outer-world struggle, but *never* can these
two make contact, to make data for the third
world. Not even God gives this possibility for
contact between inner- and outer-world
struggles; not even your heredity. Only *one*
thing—you must make *intentional contact*
between outer-world struggle and
inner-world struggle; only *then* can you make
data for the third world of Man, sometimes
called World of the Soul. Understand?

—G. I. Gurdjieff

The most pleasant and useful persons are
those who leave some of the problems of the
universe for God to worry about.

—Don Marquis

I see God as a force that guides and unites
our finest actions and sensibilities. We might
call it God because we have no other way of
explaining it. And it doesn't fit causal
rationality, where you say, "Well, this
happens, and that causes this, and this causes
that." It's a more poetic reality.

—David Byrne

Have courage for the great sorrows of life and patience for the small ones; and when you have laboriously accomplished your daily task, go to sleep in peace. God is awake.

–Victor Hugo

God knows how people ever get to that point of balance where no matter what they're into—either despair, or an excess of joy, an excess of success—that finally there is nothing more to desire and all of a sudden—Bam!—everything opens up. In other words there is satiation instead of frustration. Or satisfaction can also precipitate awareness. Or, just by accident you're walkin' down the street, and—Bam!—where is the universe? You know, it isn't chance and it isn't Times Square, it's Eternity Square all of a sudden!

–Allen Ginsberg

There will be a run on godliness, just like now there's a run on refrigerators, headphones, and fishing gear. It's going to be a matter of survival. People are going to be running to find out about God, and who are they going to run to?

–Bob Dylan

I said to Harlem street audiences that only
when mankind would submit to the One God
who created all—only then would mankind
even approach the "peace" of which so much
talk could be heard . . . but toward which so
little *action* was seen.

—Malcolm X

If you've got pain and you've got hope,
you've got a lot going for you.

—Reverend Cecil Williams

All good is gathered in three conditions. If
you cannot pass your days with what
furthers you, at least do not pass your days
with what works against you. If you cannot
befriend good people, at least do not keep
company with bad people. If you cannot give
away what is yours for God's sake, at least
do not spend your fortune on things that will
anger Him. Keep continuous repentance and
doubt that your repentance is accepted.

—Junayd

You never enjoy the world aright, till the Sea
itself floweth in your veins, till you are
clothed with the heavens and crowned with
the stars, and perceive yourself to be the sole
heir of the whole world, and more than so,
because men are in it who are every one sole
heirs as well as you.

—Thomas Traherne

Finding out where God leaves off and we
    begin
is going to wear out our shoes.

—Michael Hannon

After his enlightenment, the Buddha passed a
man on the road who was struck by the
extraordinary radiance and peacefulness of
his presence. The man stopped and asked,
"My friend, what are you? Are you a celestial
being or a god?" "No," said the Buddha. "Well
then, are you some kind of magician or
wizard?" Again the Buddha answered, "No."
"Are you an ordinary man?" "No," "Well, my
friend, what then are you?" The Buddha
replied, "I am awake."

—Jack Kornfield

All of us want a beautiful death—a brave, sweet, benevolent, manly, serene death. Or, if it is to be violent, one that carries us off in a meaningful blaze of glory. We may hope for a hero's death, or a saint's. We may want to greet death with a smile on our lips or a few choice last words, as in the cowboy movies. No one wants an accidental death, or a slow, painful death, or an unconscious, sleepwalker's death.

We want to die like men—the same way we lived.

After 35, we begin to change our outlook about longevity. We take old men as our models rather than younger men. And if we don't die gloriously young, we want to live out our golden years well—not dazed or doped, but vigorously graceful and deep.

Timothy Leary once said that we should all try to

be saints. Indeed, there are those among us who live in a state of the Miraculous—the rugged individualists who struggle to gain a greater wisdom. Saints show up at the right time in the right place, lend the right kind of hand, and say the right words. Then, with great aplomb, they do their work and go. They pass on, they die well—not a moment too soon or too late. They have lived with simplicity, just themselves and eternity, so they can smile as they slip away.

We want to live our lives as wise warriors and die as men. We may not even know what that **is** until the moment of our deaths. Then, the questions come. Have we worked to release another soul from pain? Have we opened a way that was once closed? Have we learned from the steeps and dips?

Then we can rest assured that we have lived as men and died as warriors. The rugged plain of life has been crossed. We lay down our bow. We go gladly through the small door. We stretch out our full length between the stars.

OLD AGE

Age only matters when one is aging. Now
that I have arrived at a great age, I might just
as well be twenty.

—Pablo Picasso

To an Old Fisherman

A small boat on the immense sea: who is it?

All he owns are a straw hat and raincoat.

Nobody but gulls go to visit him by the
  sandbar.

But in the autumn the fish are fat and good.

Idling, he may play his flute to the wind

Or get drunk and come home under the
  moon, a lone sail.

He might be living in the ancient tale of the
  peach spring.

What does he care what goes on in the
  world?

—Nguyen Binh Khiem

You are killing me, fish, the old man
thought. But you have a right to. Never have
I seen a greater, or more beautiful, or a
calmer or more noble thing than you,
brother. Come on and kill me. I do not care
who kills who.

—Ernest Hemingway

You've probably been wondering how I
manage to totter on at the advanced age of
eighty-two. . . . I do have a strong motivation
for keeping fit. I want to go on working as
long as I can.

—Rex Harrison

Halting of voice and limb,
flattering the mighty,
I have been made an actor in a farce.
I know not what new comedy
old age will have me dance
with these white hairs for greasepaint.

—Murari

Getting old is a fascinating thing. The older you get, the older you want to get. At 30, I couldn't have cared less, but I've jumped the hurdles to reach a point where you understand things more clearly. Getting old? With a little bit of luck, it'll happen to all of us.

—Keith Richards

Old age is the most unexpected of all the things that happen to a man.

—Leon Trotsky

Only the wisest and stupidest of men never change.

—Confucius

Beautiful Old Age

It ought to be lovely to be old
to be full of the peace that comes of
    experience
and wrinkled ripe fulfillment.

The wrinkled smile of completeness that
    follows a life
lived undaunted and unsoured with accepted
    lies.
If people lived without accepting lies
they would ripen like apples, and be scented
    like pippins
in their old age.

Soothing, old people should be, like apples
when one is tired of love.
Fragrant like yellowing leaves, and dim with
    the soft
stillness and satisfaction of autumn.

And a girl should say:
it must be wonderful to live and grow old.
Look at my mother, how rich and still she
    is!—

And a young man should think: By Jove
my father has faced all weathers, but it's
    been a life!—

                       —D. H. Lawrence

WISDOM

In rivers, the water that you touch is the last
of what has passed and the first of that which
comes; so with time present.

—Leonardo da Vinci

Look, there are no secrets. Sometimes you
walk along a beach, looking for a piece of
sand. Sometimes it's right in front of you.
You don't have to dig. The sand is the
sand—do you know what I'm saying?

—Tom Cruise

The prophet is a man who feels fiercely. God has thrust a burden upon his soul, and he is bowed and stunned at man's fierce greed. Frightful is the agony of man; no human voice can convey its full terror. Prophecy is the voice that God has lent to the silent agony, a voice to the plundered poor, to the profaned riches of the world. It is a form of living, a crossing point of God and man. God is raging in the prophet's words.

—Abraham Joshua Heschel

Yesterday's a canceled check, and tomorrow's a promissory note. But today is cash. Today is all you can really bank on.

—Adam Rich

Enjoy when you can, and endure when you must.

—Wolfgang von Goethe

Experience is not what happens to you; it is what you do with what happens to you.

—Aldous Huxley

He whose deeds exceed his wisdom, his wisdom shall endure; but he whose wisdom exceeds his deeds, his wisdom will not endure.

—Rabbin Chanina

Even a monotonously undeviating path of self-examination does not necessarily lead to a mountain of self-knowledge.

—Quentin Crisp

Mingle a little folly with your wisdom; a little nonsense now and then is pleasant.

—Horace

We should be careful to get out of an experience only the wisdom that is in it—and stop there; lest we be like the cat that sits down on a hot stove lid. She will never sit down on a hot stove lid again—and that is well; but also she will never sit down on a cold one anymore.

—Mark Twain

I don't think much of a man who is not wiser today than he was yesterday.

—Abraham Lincoln

I went to the woods because I wished to see if I could not learn what life had to teach—and not, when I came to die, discover that I had not lived.

—Henry David Thoreau

DEATH

The brave song—or death song—is a steadfast
and eloquent expression of a man who grasps
the fact of his own death. It is sung only at
times of utter desolation or when the singer
stands in the face of death. Other death songs
are composed spontaneously at the very
moment of death and are chanted with the
last breath of the dying man.

> *The odor of death,*
> *I discern the odor of death*
> *In front of my body.* (Dakota)
> —Jamake Highwater

Do not go gentle into that good night.
—Dylan Thomas

Real men don't die. It is a sign of virtue and power not to die. And if we must die, we will come back. And if we can't come back, we will fight like hell to keep from dying in the first place, telling death where to get off and determined to show courage when it comes reaping. Who knows? Maybe by this terrified show of nerve we actually do hold death off a bit.

—Roger Rosenblatt

To speculate about dying doesn't disturb me as it might some people. I never have felt that I would live to become an old man. Even before I was a Muslim—when I was a hustler in the ghetto jungle, and then a criminal in prison, it always stayed on my mind that I would die a violent death. In fact, it runs in my family. My father and most of his brothers died by violence—my father because of what he believed in. To come right down to it, if I take the kind of things in which I believe, then add to that the kind of temperament that I have, plus the one hundred per cent dedication I have to whatever I believe in—these are ingredients which make it just about impossible for me to die of old age.

—Malcolm X

Song of the Spirit
At the time of death,
when I found there was to be death,
I was very much surprised.
All was failing.
My home,
I was sad to leave it.

I have been looking far,
Sending my spirit north, south, east, and
     west,
Trying to escape from death,
But could find nothing,
No way of escape.

—Luiseño Indian song

I can't decay. I would not let myself decay.
I'm against decay. That's nature's
will—decay. I am against nature. . . . I think
nature is very unnatural. I think the only
natural things are in dreams, which nature
can't touch with decay. . . . I don't want to
see myself die. . . . All this talk about
equality. The only thing people really have in
common is that they are all going to die.

—Bob Dylan

Blessed is he who was before he became.
If you are my disciples and hear my words,
these stones will serve you.
For you have five trees in paradise;
they do not stir, summer or winter,
and their leaves do not fall off.
He who will understand them will not taste
death.

—The Secret Sayings of Jesus

If we must have cockroaches then look into
their eyes at least! Study the deaths as well as
the lives of great men. *At least do what you
want to do before you die.*

—Michael McClure

The history of the world is lost in silence.

—Jack Kerouac

A guru sat down to worship every evening, only to be disturbed by the cat who lived at the ashram. So he ordered that the cat be tied up during the evening worship. After the guru died, the cat continued to be tied up during the evening worship. And when the cat died, another cat was brought to the ashram so that it could be duly tied up during the evening worship. Centuries later, learned treatises were written by the guru's scholarly disciples on the liturgical significance of tying up a cat while worship is performed.

—Jack Kornfield

Let us all mount our horses. When I am old, I shall die. I will die at any time; I want to find out how it is. It is like going up over a divide.

—The Warrior Wants-to-Die

Man is asleep, and when he dies he wakes up.

—The Prophet Muhammad

permissions

index